"As an executive coach, I spend a lot of time helping clients build their confidence, so I'm pleased to see this book getting published! What resonates so strongly for me is Emily's combined emphasis on behaviors and mindset. I want to get the tattoo 'Why Not Me?'"

—ANTONIA BOWRING, EXECUTIVE COACH, AUTHOR

OF COACH YOURSELF: INCREASE AWARENESS,

CHANGE BEHAVIOR AND THRIVE

"Emily Jaenson's book could be just the boost you need to create the life you want. She's enthusiastic, authentic, and practical; she starts from the foundational element of self-confidence and builds from there. Her advice is solid and timely, and she delivers it like a good friend who knows all your quirks and still believes in you."

—ERIKA ANDERSEN, BUSINESS THINKER

AND BEST-SELLING AUTHOR

"I am someone who is perceived to ooze confidence. Maybe it's the fact I've beat the odds on more than one occasion or the fact I tend to be the life of the party. Truthfully, I was faking it on more than one occasion. I had a commanding presence, but I'd often come home and doubt every single decision I made that day, like, 'Why did I say that?' or 'How could I have embarrassed myself like that?' I bet you can relate. While people often mentioned my confidence as a trait they loved about me, I didn't believe it to be true. I am no longer that person. Why? Emily Jaenson and her colorful look at confidence pierced my protective exterior. From the moment she asked me to join her on the Leadership is Female podcast to her being a guest on my podcast and every conversation in between, Emily has consistently shed light on personal potential. This book is a reminder we all have the ability to do anything we set our minds to when equipped with the tools to harness our internal power. I am happy to see she had the confidence to share lessons learned and practical strategies we can apply right now to level up."

—CORINNE MILIEN, FOUNDER AND CEO OF WRK

"Emily has truly poured her heart and soul into this book, and it shows! The personal approach she has taken provides tremendous insight into how we, too, can gain and grow our own confidence and realize our dreams. Whether you are just getting started at tackling your goals or hoping to level up from where you currently are, this book will surely lay the groundwork to propel you forward."

—NICOLE WILLIAMS, WIFE AND MOM, BUSINESS
OWNER AT NICOLE WILLIAMS STATE FARM

"Emily combines emotion, humor, and straight-talk to make all of us believe and see how we can have the life we want if we invest our time in growing our confidence. Hearing her real-life experience helps put it all into perspective."

—JENNIFER MATTHEWS, MARKETING AND
BRANDING VICE PRESIDENT

"Emily Jaenson has impacted so many people through her personal journey, and this guide is an inspiration for all women in the sports field and beyond to achieve their goals. She outlines simple steps and daily actions for you to become the person you envision yourself to be."

—SHANNON KELLY, SPORTS BROADCASTER

AT NEVADA SPORTS NET

LET'S GO!

LET'S GO!

A GUIDE TO INCREASING
YOUR CONFIDENCE

*To Sparrow,
Why not you?
Let's go!*

Emily Jae

EMILY JAENSON

MANUSCRIPTS PRESS

LET'S GO!

A Guide to Increasing Your Confidence

ISBN   979-8-88504-389-2 *Paperback*

979-8-88504-388-5 *eBook*

979-8-88504-390-8 *Hardcover*

For my daughter, Elin.

Live your life confidently, boldly, and in a way that's true to who you are. Never let anyone stand in the way of your dreams.

Contents

"Be so good they won't forget you."

—EMILY JAENSON

INTRODUCTION

Confidence Is a Skill

WHY DID I WRITE THIS BOOK?

In the spring of 2022, I hit the stage of TEDx in Reno, Nevada. I had a message to share on increasing confidence. Through my journey of growing this skill set, I went from *can't dial the phone to talk to a stranger to order a pizza* kind of shy to *talking on the TEDx stage in front of thousands to create a video for hopefully millions to watch.* I realized if I could use these steps to grow my confidence, you could, too.

On that day in May, at the TEDx event, I was on the schedule to speak second to last, meaning I would spend the entire day in the convention center waiting to speak. Accomplished individuals surrounded me like best-selling authors, doctors, and a comedian with millions of followers and a Netflix special on the way. I could have let negative thoughts creep in. That would, however, have been so counter to my talk. I was speaking on confidence! I won the spot onstage, and I would do my best. I had set my mind to it.

I began to look around and most of the conversation among the speakers was a discussion around their nerves. "I'm so nervous!" "This is so nerve-wracking!" "I'm not sure I am ready!" The list went on and on. I felt an urge to join in the conversation before my brain quickly reminded me this conversation was not only unproductive but detrimental to my performance.

I decided I would have fun. I'd worked my butt off to memorize my talk with an impactful delivery. I needed to get away, but I couldn't go home and get distracted. I found a room in the back of the convention center with a mirror, and I practiced like I would perform—full out—smile, energy, volume, and delivery at one-hundred percent. I pulled myself out of the speaker environment filled with nervous energy and put myself into a space with the confidence I wanted to give the audience. I had rehearsed, and it was showtime. I asked myself, *Why spend my day in misery when I can make this process fun?* I would practice what I preached.

My turn came around in the late afternoon. I was mic'ed up and hit the stage running with a huge smile on my face. The audience sat up. I watched them watching me. I saw smiles, applause, and heads nodding along to my points. Realizing I nailed it, my eleven minutes on stage ended, and I threw up my hands in celebration. Why not wave? Why not enjoy this moment? I did it.

I practiced the confidence I taught and did something that would have surprised my sixteen-year-old self, who couldn't order a pizza. I spoke on a big stage, in front of a big audience, and I loved it.

The work I put in to grow my confidence had paid off. One year later, my talk had over three million views on YouTube.[1] The world responded that yes, we could all strive to achieve more of our dreams if we had greater confidence to stay in pursuit.

WHO SHOULD YOU READ THIS BOOK?

This book is for you now. Who you are today. You may be in a great spot. You may have achieved more than your Aunt Sue ever thought possible, but the drive within you still burns. You just need the encouragement, a road map, and new guide rails installed. You'd love direction on increasing your confidence in a world that seems to keep growing around you, making you feel small and insignificant in your daily life.

The exhaustive list of who you are is multi-hyphenate. It could include being a mother, father, wife, husband, partner, friend, sister, volunteer, coach, Uber driver, and an all-star employee. You get ideas for new pursuits everywhere you look. You heard a new podcast. You saw your friend have success. Your coworker just got a promotion. You want it all but end up with a notebook filled with ideas and no action. Looking at the list of things you should do just makes you feel worse, and your confidence falls down another rung on the ladder of life.

Despite this list, if you are like me, you are looking for a way to level up. You made the list in the first place with the intention of using it to better your life.

Life is busy, competitive, and can feel crowded. Confidence to achieve our goals can chip away in the passing of a day. We can't commit to considering one percent more when our goal is the size of an elephant. I heard several years ago, "How do you eat an elephant?" The answer: "One bite at a time." We can't look at the whole goal and try to achieve it all at once. Incrementally, over time, we work a little each day, and before we know it, we look back, and we've come so freaking far.

If you are stuck and can't find the motivation, this book is for you. The fire inside of you is barely a big enough flame at the end of a match to light a candle, but it's burning, nonetheless.

This book is here to teach you the necessary behaviors to confidently pursue your wildest dreams. Are you in?

To grow our confidence, we have to fight against a common thought, "Not me!" and turn that into the opportunity of, "Why not me?"

Some people will look at others and think, "She's born with it. She's had a leg up, a predestined chance for success, an opportunity I don't have. She can get ahead in life easier than me. She's got it. I don't."

Let's be honest, some people do get a leg up depending on how financially stable their families were when they were growing up, where they grew up, or who their parents knew. However, I am here to tell you anyone can succeed on their terms if they develop one skill—confidence.

While some are born with connections, privilege, or access, the stories we remember the most are about the people who weren't born with any of these things.

These words changed my life. "Why not *you*?" Seriously, why not you? We hear incredible stories of perseverance every day. Of athletes who apply tremendous willpower and beat all odds to win the biggest of games. Women who become astronauts. Gold medalists who grew up in poverty. CEOs who got there with no connections. So, I'll ask again, why not you?

Some of us have larger-than-life goals like going to space, winning a gold medal, or founding a billion-dollar company. While I believe becoming more confident can help you achieve *anything you set your mind* to, this book is for:

- the person who wants to run their first 5k
- the young professional who is applying for their first promotion
- the woman in her early forties who is finally ready to apply to law school
- the middle manager who is ready to pitch the boss on why he or she will be the next VP
- the girl just accepted to do a TEDx with stage fright
- the woman who wants to write a book or simply publish her first LinkedIn post to celebrate her individual success

Without pursuing our goals, micro or larger-than-life, we are stuck. We live in a world without inspiration, and each day is more monotonous than the last. It's difficult to do hard things, but when we become more confident, we won't let negative thoughts stop us from chasing our dreams.

WHAT WILL YOU LEARN FROM THIS BOOK?

Part I, Behaviors, contains the introduction and chapters 1–5. This section will inspire you and motivate you to become a more confident person, and this will change your life. You'll go from stuck to unstoppable. If you feel passed over or like you are not living up to your potential, these chapters will work to change your mind so you can consider living a big life, fulfilling your potential in pursuit of your passions. Right now, you may lack the confidence to even speak your goals aloud, but buried deep down inside of you is this little voice, a whisper, saying, "Let's go." You'll finish this section, and your mind will be open to the most important idea of your life. You will say, "Why not me?" when you speak your biggest goal.

Part II, Mindset, contains Chapters 6–10. I will teach you the mindset, tactics, strategies, and the next right thing to reach your biggest (or smallest) goals. Let's start. Imagine where you'll be if you apply confident behaviors and take the right next step every day. It will be uncomfortable in your Payless pumps or inexpensive suit, but repeating practiced behaviors will change your attitude to one of greater confidence. One step leads to another and another, and you are on your way to achieving what you set out to do. I'll help you make the most out of each achievement so you can create the life of your dreams on your terms. Your life, your job, your body, your heart, your mind, and your community potentially will become what you've always wanted. All we need to do is take the next right step together.

Part III, Action, contains chapters 11–15. Have you ever heard the phrase "Bet on yourself?" I love it. It puts the ball in your court and leaves no one to blame but yourself. A lot of people hate this. They ask, "Who will I be if I don't have an excuse or someone to get in my way of progress? I'll have to count on myself to get it done!" Well, that's the point. If you want to change your life, you are the only person who can do it. If you want to reach your goals, big and small, you must take action. If you want to lead a better, more purposeful life on your terms, then take *action* on your dreams utilizing your growing confidence.

This book covers over twenty years of my life, collected knowledge from over one hundred interviews on the *Leadership is Female* podcast,[2] and endless reading, studying, and action to create these fifteen chapters. It's a considerable amount of information, but my hope is it does not overwhelm you but inspires you. I hope you see that through these examples, growth is possible for all of us. Can you see yourself in these stories? I hope you find inspiration and opportunities to practice what you've learned so you can experience the kind of change you'd like in your life. All we need to do is take the next right step to grow our confidence together. So, let's go!

PART I

BEHAVIORS

CHAPTER 1

Find Your Why

———

"You really should not be wearing those shoes." I turned around to see an older man with a significant beer gut standing behind me on the concourse. "A woman in your condition" appeared to be missing from his comment.

I was nine months pregnant with my first son, and it was August of baseball season. I had worked sixty-five games on nights and weekends, plus full forty-hour weeks in the office to get through a Triple-A Minor League Baseball season, and I really was not having it. No thanks for the comments from the peanut gallery.

I turned around on three-and-a-half-inch wedge heels, looked him in the face, and said, "I think I'll be okay," and briskly walked away down the concourse.

When I announced my pregnancy at work at thirteen weeks, I was nervous as hell. My heart was racing, my palms sweaty, and my brain racking with *what-ifs,* which was completely confusing since this should have been a celebration. My husband and I were bringing a new life into the world, and I could not have been more excited to start this next chapter.

In the back of my mind, it meant change for me. I had a plan and a trajectory at work, and now, caring for a little person would shift my priorities. Would I be the same? Would my goals point in the same direction? How would my confidence and willpower waiver when a tiny human keeps me up all night?

Other people's opinions affronted me on every level. Leaving my boss's office after telling him the news about my pregnancy and plans to return to work following my baby's birth, the CFO followed me to my cubicle. He promptly announced his wife had plans to return to work following the birth of their child but didn't, and she had stayed home for the past thirteen years.

My response was, "Good for her! Great for your family! But my plan is to return to work." I thought, *Wow, I wish you would keep your opinions to yourself and let me decide what to do with my life!*

HOW MY VISION FOR CHANGE BECAME MY REALITY

While working in corporate partnership sales for the baseball team, I was climbing the ladder. I juggled a multitude of meetings and seamlessly delivered perfectly crafted advertising decks showcasing the optimal placement for company logos in the park. I had reached my annual sales goals just after the start of the season in late April, which would have been a huge relief, except a big part of our job was not only showing up for the nine-to-five sales hours but for the baseball games, too.

This meant many days looked like working from nine a.m. to ten p.m.

I had my game day polo, maternity work pants, and a three-and-a-half-inch wedge. I walked more than 14,000 steps a day, and most days, I grabbed a workout during lunch at the gym down the street in downtown Reno.

I wanted to prove myself at work. I wanted to stay fit for myself and my baby. I wanted to do everything my non-pregnant coworkers did and more.

No excuses and no feet up with bonbons for my growing baby belly. PS, the bonbon joke is still alive for pregnant women everywhere.

I wanted to show everyone who would watch that women can do anything they set their mind to, including working thirteen-hour days in heels. I wanted to meet my sales goals and make the commission my family so desperately needed.

My Why for doing this was beginning to form, and it felt different than the personal achievement I'd reached at other points in my life. The feeling was deeper and driven by someone other than me.

After game number seventy-two in early September, the final game of the season, I drove the thirty-seven miles home to our house in rural Nevada and called my husband from the road in tears.

He said, "Why are you crying?"

My answer was, "Because I freaking did it."

My goal was to work the requirements. Take no shortcuts, never leave early, or make excuses as to why I couldn't do the job. I didn't want special accommodations, and my son cooperating safely inside my belly was a blessing. He was healthy, I was healthy, and we did it together.

Working in sports is a competitive industry, and job openings in a front office are few and far between, especially the higher you climb. For women, this statistic is even tougher. "At any given time, women comprised between 20–34 percent of senior professional team administrators," according to the Women's Sports Foundation.[1] Teams of less than a few hundred are running sports organizations worth billions in the majors, and fewer than fifty run teams worth tens of millions in the minors.

I knew I was having a boy. Being a woman working with a bunch of men, I wanted to prove to myself and show my son that women can do anything. He would know nothing different, and when it came to a day when he saw a pregnant woman standing on the concourse at a baseball game, he would not question her shoe choice. He would think to himself, "Good for her," and move on to his seat. Working women in any *condition* would be something he'd seen his whole life.

This was my Why: to set an example for the next generation and to show them what was possible. Women wouldn't have to choose between being a mom and pursuing a career, and men wouldn't think twice about her capabilities.

Two weeks postseason that September, my son, all seven pounds, one ounce of him, came into this world, changing my life forever. He was my reason for showing up, pushing myself, and achieving more than I thought possible.

I brought my newborn baby home from the hospital and started my two-week work vacation. I only had ten days of paid time off and then had arranged to take my maternity leave in my own way, which allowed me to keep earning and keep climbing.

I had pitched a twenty-hour work week from home before telecommuting was really a thing. This was 2013. I knew I'd need to show up in person as soon as possible, and I agreed to do so for client meetings after six weeks. I needed my teammates to help me in the interim. If I had a new business meeting, they would go in my stead and make my pitch to the client to sponsor the baseball team the following year. I needed to ask for help, and I needed them to say yes. They were my teammates, and we'd need to work together to reach our annual sponsorship goal. I promised to repay the support in any way I could by, most importantly, landing new business so we'd all achieve our bonuses.

I read all the books about how to be a good mother, including a very important one about feeding your baby. Magnus was on a quick schedule. After those two weeks of new baby bliss, he started napping on schedule with me scheduling sales calls in between. He was an absolute champ, and our routine allowed me to get in exactly four hours of work per day so I could keep working on my dream and earning money for our family.

I was about six weeks into maternity leave when I landed a second meeting, this time in-person, with a prospective sponsor.

I scheduled for Magnus to start daycare after the holidays, but when I wrote my own maternity leave policy, I stated I'd take meetings at six weeks. The diligent work over the six-week time frame had resulted in an in-person meeting opportunity.

I was lucky. My work was somewhat flexible, but only because I was producing revenue. They saw my efforts and rewarded my nontraditional work environment. The team's accounting manager, a woman who had her own grandchildren, gladly agreed to watch Magnus while I went to the meeting.

I dropped him at the ballpark and proceeded to the credit union to meet with the marketing manager. In an hour, I knew I had sold my idea, and the next week, she called to say they were in. It was the most joy I had ever felt for something I accomplished at work and one of the larger deals I had closed to date. I closed a deal at nearly eight weeks postpartum.

I thought the goal was to make it through the season pregnant, but now I knew the goal was to thrive after becoming a mom. Thrive at work, at home, and as a mother. Women can do it all, and I would join that club. I returned to work in January, and my boss called me into the office. I was all nerves. What was this meeting about? I literally just arrived!

The meeting was to award me a promotion and a raise.

My Why only continued to grow when I began to work harder to achieve my goals. My Why was about showing my son that leadership is female. Women work in sports. Mommy achieved her goals just like Daddy did. Women can achieve anything they set their minds and effort toward. I had found my Why, and the seed planted during pregnancy only grew larger post-birth. The Why sprouted branches and gave me ideas for what I could do next. The Why inspired new goals.

Your Why picks you up when you are down. Your Why helps you to set and achieve new goals. Without a Why or a purpose, you will be stuck. No one can define this for you. Your Why can be for yourself, your family, and your legacy; you define it.

Why do you do what you do? Find your purpose. If you have that north star, it is so much easier to show up for your goals.

FINDING MY WHY CHANGED EVERYTHING
Five years later, in 2018, my Why experienced a palpable shift. I had earned the General Manager role back at that same baseball team. A tagline adjacent to the job description read, "First Female General Manager in Triple-A Baseball in nearly Twenty Years."

I didn't know what to do with that tagline. I had earned this role because of the way I could lead a business, not because I was a woman. The team was not looking to make news or gain notoriety for hiring a woman. I was equally resentful of the attention and aware of the honor.

Thirty total teams comprise the Triple-A level. I was one of thirty general managers at the level and the only woman. Truly, the only woman in the room. My unique skill set has allowed me to earn this role. Suddenly, the nonlinear path was the only one that could have gotten me this job. I believe if I had gone the traditional route of sticking to a team, it might have taken me even longer to get to that email in 2018 that said, "What would it take to get you back to Reno to be our general manager?"

I was a jill-of-all-trades, having worked in ticket sales, not-for-profit and community partnerships, partnerships sales, and major events. If you knew me, you would understand I could do it all and had hit a home run in the industry with this job offer. Now, I couldn't mess it up, and the pressure I felt was palpable. It wasn't just my career on the line. I was laying the groundwork for every woman after.

Six months after starting the job, I was at Baseball Winter Meetings in Las Vegas, Nevada, where executives from all 160 Minor League Teams would gather for a three-day conference. Our colleagues in Major League Baseball were there, too, meeting, negotiating, and attempting to sign the next great player.

I received an invitation to speak on a panel to a room full of "Women in Baseball" where they asked questions like:

- "What do you think about imposter syndrome?"
- "How do you achieve work-life balance?"
- "What was the key to earning your role?"

Microphone in hand, they placed me on a stage, and instead of freezing and letting my thumping heartbeat stifle my voice, I spoke.

I shared all my thoughts and opinions, including asking, "What the hell is imposter syndrome?" which gave the room a good laugh. It was also the reason I knew I didn't have it or would never recognize it. I could do anything I set my mind to, and I knew I had earned the title.

Leaving the stage, a line of women greeted me. One after another, they said to me, "We didn't know we could be a GM at the Triple-A level until we saw you."

This came to me as a shock and as an epiphany. The quote from Marian Wright Edelman rang in my head, "You can't be what you can't see."[2]

My Why had grown branches from its trunk to include my son, providing for my family, and serving my team. It included leading others forward in their careers by setting an example of what was possible.

HOW TO FIND YOUR WHY

In an interview with Odessa Jenkins, named one of the "Most Influential and Powerful Women in Sports" by *Sports Illustrated*, she discusses how to get to your Why. Jenkins said, "Getting to your Why is easy. Think, if you have all the resources you need financially, money is not an issue, and you can solve all of your natural problems, what is the first thing you do because you want it? What is the thing you do every day because you want to do it."[3]

Jenkins went on to say, "Here are things I would do every year, every month, every week, every day and take that list and prioritize it to keep yourself in line with your purpose. You know how you impact the world, but it gets muddy with the stuff you have to do so you can do what you want to do."[4]

We all have responsibilities day to day, but Odessa Jenkins's point was that in addition to taking care of your basic needs, you must always locate your North Star, your purpose, and your Why to live a fulfilled life. You may never be so rich that you can ignore what you have to do to be financially secure, but you will likely be in a circumstance where you can choose between what you have to do and what you want to do. Don't forget that option.

She added, "Women focus so much on what we have to do because society sets so much of that for us: you have to wear this, look this way, work here, sound this way. So much of our culture tells us what we have to do, so we can't make sense of what we want to do."[5]

She broke the mold. After learning to play football against boys from a very young age, she made it her mission to create opportunities for women where none existed, like cofounding the Women's National Football Conference.

Consistently focusing on your Why can get you to your ultimate success because people are successful when they are doing what they want to do. Jenkins's final advice is to "Never lose sight of what you want to do because that ties into your Why."[6]

Another strategy to finding your Why is thinking about the impact you can have through living to your purpose. Jackie Carson, former head coach of women's basketball at Furman University and now the Atlantic Coast Conference's Senior Associate Commissioner for Women's Basketball, said, "I felt like my voice was having such an impact. I never felt like I wanted to stop."[7]

Jackie's initial hesitation in sharing her voice came from not fully understanding her Why. It wasn't until she joined boards and connected with other female coaches, specifically young female Black coaches who wanted to get into the ranks of college coaching, that she knew she could make an impact. She found a statistic that women of color are less likely hired and more likely fired quicker from their roles. This statistic became the foundation of Jackie's Why.

Jackie said, "We have to be better, win quickly, and add value to the university in addition to winning games."[8] Because of this knowledge and her position, she identified her Why and has made a larger impact beyond her team to include supporting other female coaches and their programs and encouraging more women to enter the field.

On episode seventy-eight of the *Leadership is Female* Podcast, "Do Something That Means Something," we learned that Shauna Griffiths, former NBA team employee, Nike associate, and advertising agency exec, founded a media platform, SLG Impact, where her podcast and blog focus on elevating the voices of diverse, authentic leaders who share a commitment to creating positive impact. "I believe you only have one life, and it is part of the responsibility to lead that life in a way that you are truly happy and not waste any of your days. Stand in your strength and find your voice. Get over yourself and get over your insecurities. Realize it is not easy to put yourself forward and have confidence in yourself in moments where you want to change. You might get into analysis paralysis. As much as you can, imperfectly, take the next step, and learn as you go. It won't be perfect, but you must get off the rock."[9]

Realizing many people were not living up to their potential and were not happy about it inspired Shauna to follow her purpose and her Why in helping other leaders level up. She wanted to do her part to change that fact and used her platform and her network to help leaders connect to programs and content to support their journey to more. Through this work, she's created an impactful platform and undoubtedly a ripple effect on the lives of countless driven professionals.

From another perspective, accomplished author and speaker Simon Sink has a famous TEDx Talk that has now turned into a book on the topic of finding your Why, where he says this: "Your Why is the thing you give to the world. And amongst your closest and best friends, it is the space you fill in their lives."[10]

He gives us this advice for finding *your* Why:

1. Find a friend you love and ask them this simple question, "Why are we friends?"
2. Then, "What specifically is it about *me* that you'd be there for me no matter what?"
3. They will start to describe you.
4. Play devil's advocate and ask them *specifically*, "What is it about me?"
5. They will start describing you and then they will describe them and the way you make them feel, and you will get an indication through goosebumps or chills that they've said it and you recognized it.

The only place to start is with Why. Before you turn a single additional page in this book, start with this exercise. We can't become a more confident person if we don't know why we want to become one. We can't employ our willpower to chase our dreams if we don't have a reason. Start with Why, and the rest of the work will begin to fall into place.

In an article entitled "Knowing Your Why Is Good for You" by The Bronfenbrenner Center for Translation Research at Cornell University, "Research demonstrated that a sense of purpose boosts well-being. The center's study followed almost 2,000 middle-aged adults to find out if having a sense of purpose helped them to better cope with life's daily stresses. Study participants rated their own sense of purpose on a seven-point scale. Then they completed daily interviews with researchers about stressful experiences, if they had any physical symptoms, and reported on their emotions."[11]

The findings were not surprising, "Those who reported feeling a stronger sense of purpose in their lives were significantly less likely to experience negative emotions, such as being nervous, hopeless, lonely, or irritable, as a result of the daily stress. They were also more likely to report feeling positive emotions, such as being calm and peaceful, cheerful, active, and confident. In addition, they were significantly less likely to report physical symptoms, such as fatigue or having a headache or cough."[12]

Research proves a strong sense of purpose in your life can help you better handle stress, regulate your emotions, and drive you to greater achievement.

LET'S FIND YOUR WHY—ASK YOURSELF:
- Self-Reflection and finding your Why:
  - Think back to when you were a kid. What were your examples of work? Who around you achieved all of their goals? How did you start to find out what is possible? How did this shape you?
  - What do you still believe? What don't you believe any longer?
- What do you commit to?
  - What was the last commitment you made?
  - How did you decide to make that commitment?
  - What do you do today and each day to make sure you are fulfilling that commitment?

- Give yourself the gift of books and podcasts, and curate your social media accounts to support your ambitions. Fuel your brain with the good stuff and surround yourself with the voices that will help you to achieve your goals.
- What is your Why?
  - Where do you want to make a difference?
  - What will you achieve when you do?
  - What does success look like for you when you are following your Why?

TOP FOUR TAKEAWAYS:

Finding your Why is crucial when pursuing a goal because it provides you with a deep sense of purpose, motivation, and clarity.

1. **Motivation:** When you have a clear understanding of why you want to achieve a particular goal, it creates a strong internal motivation that keeps you going, especially during challenging times. Your Why acts as a driving force that propels you forward and gives you the strength to persist in the face of obstacles.

2. **Clarity:** Knowing your Why helps you gain clarity on what you truly want to achieve and why it matters to you. It helps you define your priorities and align your actions with your values. This clarity enables you to make better decisions, set meaningful goals, and stay focused on what really matters.

3. **Resilience and Commitment:** Inevitably, you will face setbacks and obstacles along the way. But when you have a compelling Why, it provides you with the resilience and determination to keep going despite these challenges.

Your Why acts as a reminder of the greater purpose you are working toward, helping you bounce back from setbacks, and continue your journey. Knowing your Why strengthens your commitment toward your goal. It creates a sense of personal investment and dedication that increases your level of commitment. This commitment helps you stay disciplined and committed to taking consistent action toward your goal, even when it gets tough or inconvenient.

4. **Fulfillment:** Achieving a goal without a clear Why may leave you feeling empty or unsatisfied. When you know your Why, reaching your goal becomes more than just a box to tick off—it becomes a meaningful and fulfilling accomplishment. Your Why gives you a sense of purpose and satisfaction, making the journey toward your goal more rewarding and meaningful.

CHAPTER 2

Build Intention

———

I was the drunken employee. This was long before I found my Why. Straight out of college sorority life into an office with a little cubicle surrounded by new college grads, I took on the same persona I had in college, *activities chair,* except without the filter for my new workplace. I found the bars in Lincoln Park with two-dollar hamburgers on Tuesday and one-dollar beer and indulged my nine-dollars-an-hour salary alongside my new friends. I didn't know when to quit—the beer was so cheap—and often ended up back in my swivel chair the next morning hungover with a stale smell of beer permeating my pores.

During our lunch hour at the office, I came up with a brilliant idea and told all of my fellow interns around the table we would have a case race! I'd organize us into groups of two with our preassigned accountability partner to participate in this competition held at my apartment.

During our nine-month internship with the Chicago Bulls, our accountability partner was a fellow intern who sat in the cubicle next to us. Our job was to push each other to be excellent every day, including making more calls, asking for sales, and cheering each other on when we received a "no" from a prospect.

Each pair in this intern class was male and female. Justin was my accountability partner for the internship and the case race. He was from Wisconsin, so I automatically thought his birthplace, along with my genealogy (Norwegian by way of Wisconsin), would help us win the case race, no doubt.

Word spread, and our boss found out. He pulled me aside and asked when I'd planned to hold this event. "Thursday," I replied.

He asked I move it to a weekend so as not to have his entire ticket sales work force show up hungover on a workday, but it just didn't work for the group's schedule. I ignored the request, and the entire class came to my Chicago brownstone apartment on Thursday night after work. Each brought an eighteen-pack of beer. I don't think I even told my roommates we'd have visitors as fourteen interns piled into our living room.

I took it seriously. It was a race. Hello, competitive personality! I employed every bit of my competitiveness to win, urging Justin to drink faster. Justin was, and still is, a smart, dedicated, talented guy who agreed to play along but was more mature than me and could see this was a bad idea. I could see his looks of uncertainty, and although I was nearly half his size, I drank more beers than him. Two hours into the beer-guzzling event, many wiser than me had given up. With only two teams left, Justin and I and one other accountability pair finished the very last beer at the same time—a tie.

Then it hit me. I was falling over drunk. The plan was to go to the neighborhood bar, like we needed more drinks, and I stumbled into and then out of Wills Northwoods Inn on Racine in the heart of South Lakeview. I promptly passed out in my bedroom without even changing my clothes.

When my alarm went off the next morning, I felt drunk and hungover at the same time. I stunk, and not even the hottest water could wash the smell of beer away. I was running late and called another intern to come and pick me up so I would not have to take the forty-five-minute EL and bus ride out to the United Center. He reluctantly did, and I felt like a complete mess. It was not the morning I envisioned, which included a shiny "Case Race Champion" trophy riding along with me to work with the employees cheering me on as I entered the building.

When I took my seat, no fist bumps or smiles surrounded me. My intern friends were getting ready to start our sales job and do the work meant for Friday. Most nursed hangovers like me. I struggled to decide if two hours of fun was worth the nine hours of agony we'd all experience in our office chairs, not to mention the disappointment I knew my boss felt toward me.

My world twisted. Feeling stuck in college mode, I thought I'd eat grilled cheese at the sorority house the next morning, hungover with my sisters. I realized I was in the real world. I was embarrassed. I cringe when I think about it today. My boss asked me not to host a case race at my house on a work night, and I did it anyway. I showed up the next day hungover and looked like crap when I had work to do.

I learned a valuable lesson that morning. It was time to grow up. It was time to change. The person I wanted to be was no longer the drunken sorority girl cheerleader. She was serious about her job and did great work. One day, she'd be in charge. She could still go out with her colleagues at work, but she was in control. It was time for me to change.

I wish this had happened overnight. I continued to have more missteps than I could count. It didn't always involve a case race. Sometimes, it was letting a friend down, letting myself down, or not doing my best work. I was in transition for many years.

Give yourself the grace to become the person you were meant to be. The person who you want to be. Along with grace comes a healthy dose of patience, too. I remember being in my early twenties and wondering how long it would take to be a manager, then a boss, then run a company. Maybe a few years? Ha! I wanted it all and right away, but I didn't understand how much time it would take to up-skill, become an adult, and create the mentality necessary to elevate my career. It meant a lot of work and was all much further down the road than I had envisioned.

In an article written for *Psychology Today*, author Thomas Webb, PhD, discussed building a bridge between intention and action. Dr. Webb provided specific types of action planning that involved forming an if-then plan or "implementation intention."[1]

Dr. Webb went on to describe, "If-then planning was first described by Peter Gollwitzer and involved identifying an opportunity in which to act (in the if-part of the plan), deciding in advance how to respond to that opportunity (in the then-part of the plan), and then linking the opportunity and response together."[2]

So, if your intention was to wake up early to work out, followed by getting to work before everyone else to get a jump on the day, you need to identify what might be stopping you from currently taking this action. Staying up too late or watching too much TV? Maybe you never stopped working the night before and checked your email late into the evening, which made you feel this extra effort wasn't worth it. Then, when you roll in late to the office each morning, you feel like you are behind the ball.

The next step is how you respond to the opportunity. In this case, it could be action, like going to bed earlier or thinking about how good you will feel starting your day with a workout and settling into work before the day starts. Dr. Webb said, "The idea is that, by specifying in advance how to respond, the person does not need to deliberate at the critical moment."[3]

You have decided on the opportunity and understand its benefit, so when your alarm goes off and you feel the temptation to hit snooze, look down at the exercise shoes and outfit you set out the night before and quickly decide how good you will feel about yourself when you accomplish your intention.

DEVELOPING FIVE AREAS OF INTENTION

Having perspective on past events is easy when you're looking back. Looking forward is the unknown and requires thought to continue goal-oriented progress in your life. Here are some steps I have laid out to help me feel intentional with my time. These five areas of intention: *wake up, build, pursue, boundaries*, and *believe* changed everything for me. I evolved from a drunken employee to a girl going after her goals in a healthy, fulfilling way.

1. WAKE UP: YOUR PREPAREDNESS ROUTINE.

Do you know those people (maybe it's you) who slide into a chair in a meeting and check their phones or frantically search on their laptops? Yep, you know a calendar alert went off, and they reported for duty but did not know what exactly they showed up for. Don't let that be you.

We have heard the advice time and time again that if you are the most prepared one in the room, often they'll pursue your idea. Are you prepared? Do you know why you are there?

- Before you start your next day of work, either the night before or the morning of, review your calendar. Plot all you've signed yourself up for on your calendar—bonus points for color coding.
- What meetings are you attending? What is the agenda? Do you know how you will contribute, and do you know why they invited you? Hopefully, the answer to all of these questions is yes, and if so, get to work thinking about how you will contribute to a resolution, idea, or create

movement in the project. Be the most prepared in the room.

- Fill in the rest of that whitespace on your calendar with all the work you have to get done. Be realistic and command your day. You'll feel so much better at the conclusion of your work with an openness and freedom to take time for yourself or your family when you know you have everything done you needed to do. You'll have approached your time with intention, which is a great feeling.

2. BUILD: BUILD YOUR COMMUNITY.

Finding a mentor sounds difficult, like searching for the pot of gold at the end of a rainbow. You've got a full-time job and not a second to look. The worst part is this pot of gold person needs to help you. You're searching for something hard to find and need to ask for help! This endeavor is not something you look forward to and may even dread, which is why you have not done it yet. However, mentorship is essential to building your community. Entire books address the topic, so I'll share some ideas about mentorship to make it feel more attainable.

- Look internally. Is your direct supervisor at work a person who takes pride in watching his or her staff grow? Maybe that person has a little extra time for you if you show an interest in learning from his or her experience. Look across the departments in your organization. Do you know another leader you admire? Pick your head up for opportunities inside your company because availability is likely easier to coordinate if you work in the same building. You'll have a chance for recognition as a standout among your peers when you are spending time learning from internal management.

- Find an association. My first real mentoring relationship came from a group called Women in Baseball. I know plenty more of these resource groups exist in every industry. Get involved in the association. If a structured mentorship program is available, apply. If not, start showing up and look for someone in the room with more experience than you and get to know that person. People do like to give advice. Be open, helpful, and curious, and develop that relationship.

Inside your community, start to think about expanding your vocabulary to include these two concepts: Board of Directors and Sponsors.

- Board of Directors: A group of colleagues and friends who help guide you in your decision-making in your career. This is informal and more about how you think about and use these relationships. It can include someone who works on your team at work, a former colleague, a friend from school, a person you have volunteered with, someone on your intramural basketball team who has their life together and is always willing to share over a beer (not half a case of beer) after a game. You have relationships in your life with people who have similar goals as you to build their careers. Reach out to them when you are making a decision. Ask for advice. People like to help. Talk through it. Let this Board of Directors grow and support you in the most organic way.
- Sponsors: A group of people who know you do great work and will mention your name in rooms you are not in.

This is the group that will get you your next opportunity, award, mention, or promotion. The quickest way to get sponsors is first to do great work and ensure that people know what you can do in a humble way. The second step is letting them know you are ready for an opportunity. Reach out to let them know if you are looking for a new job, tell them you did something great, and never forget to congratulate them on their great work, promotion, or significant life event.

As you build your community, your life will change. The working world will open up, and you won't feel so lonely in your current position or, even worse, stuck. Keep in touch with these groups of people, and don't feel like the only way you will find them is by attending a networking event. Think bigger and deeper and build your community organically by being a great friend, colleague, and employee.

3. PURSUE: PURSUE YOUR GOALS WITH EXCELLENCE AND SET NEW GOALS FROM THE TOP.

Walking aimlessly through your year is the worst thing you can do. You need to call your shot annually. When I was a case racing intern, I certainly had ideas of what I wanted to do. Get a full-time job, earn more money, and run a half marathon. It stopped there. I didn't write them down. I didn't have a plan. I just had them in my mind and worked each day in a way I thought would make them come true. I never thought through the second part: if I achieve them, what's next?

- To set appropriate goals, you need to start with reflection. I feel like this gives you a running start on your goal setting. If you can reflect on all you have accomplished in the year prior, you are much more primed to think of a mix of both big and confidently achievable goals for the next year. To pursue your goals, you must first reflect.
- Then, set goals for both personal and professional achievement. Separate the two. Yes, we live 360, 3D lives as humans, which is why you need goals in both areas. You also need to write these out separately so your mind can wrap around the fact you've got space for both. Ink it. Share it. Create at least three in each category of personal and professional.
- Halfway through the year, revisit. If you have checked these goals off, high-five yourself, pop some bubbly, call your mom, get a massage, and do something to celebrate. Commemorate the moment and enjoy your success. You called your shot, and you freaking did it.
- Then, do the exercise again. What did you accomplish in the first half of the year, and what do you want to do in the second half? Don't waste half your year coasting.

You might be thinking this explanation sounds exhausting, and your new friend Emily is running you into the ground, collecting gold stars. But goals require you to stay the course, and they also create something very, very special for you. Purpose.

Start thinking about your goals here, and in Chapter 12, we will dive deeper into setting your goals to get you to the next level.

4. BOUNDARIES. HOW AND WHERE TO SET BOUNDARIES IS IMPERATIVE TO YOUR SUCCESS. YOU DON'T HAVE TO BE AVAILABLE FOR EVERYONE AT EVERY TURN.

You can't *do it all* if you say yes to everything. There is simply not enough time in the day, space in your brain, or patience in your heart. You have to set boundaries.

My good friend, colleague, Personal Board of Directors member, and guest on the *Leadership is Female* Podcast, Jenna Byrnes, repeated this quote, "If it's not a hell yes, it's a hell *no*." [4] If the request for your participation does not elicit "hell yes," (with the exception of activities and projects you have to do because you are paid to them by your employer) then it's a no. Think committee member, volunteering, chaperone, coach, attending a meeting with no expected outcomes, or a trip with the family to a location you have no desire to see and limited vacation time. The list is endless, and we can all think of things we said yes to and, in the end, would rather have done a million other things than pretzelled ourselves into attendance.

Early in my leadership role, I said yes to everything. Boards, committees, reading to school children, meetings with people who wanted to meet me but didn't fulfill my goals at work, networking events, breakfasts, you name it. I filled my calendar and, in the middle, squeezed in my office work and time with family. I sped down the highway twenty mph over the speed limit, sweating with nerves that I'd be late again, trying to get to my next commitment. My priorities were crap, and I was doing everything on everyone else's agenda and not being the productive leader, wife, or mother I had envisioned myself to be.

One word changed that. "No." It's a complete sentence. It usually doesn't owe much explanation. You can soften it with, "not at this time, can you follow up next quarter?" Most of the time, that person who asked you to do something won't follow up with you in three months. If that's the case, was it really that important in the first place? Trust your gut. Say no when the ask does not serve your priorities.

5. BELIEVE. YOU'VE GOT ALL THE TOOLS TO MAKE IT HAPPEN.
Look how far I've come. I was a rural kid with dreams sidelined by partying and a college hangover. However, I internally kept the drive to keep working and a fire in my belly that repaired several flat tires on the twisty road of my career. I had the confidence in myself to keep putting one foot in front of the other.

- When I got scared, I used an old tactic from my days in sports, "Three, two, one... go." I'd count myself into an activity I was nervous about starting, just like in a race. Counting would get me started, and momentum would keep me going.
- I'd look back at how far I'd come—utilizing the rearview mirror as a tool and an inspiration.
- I'd look around me and notice all the gifts I had in my life. My health, a working car, a bank account, a blue sky, work clothes to show up and look the part. All along the way, I acknowledged my gifts.

You can too, believe it. You have it all. It's all inside you. What you don't have yet, you have a brain that can learn. You have a mouth to speak in conversation to gain friends and ask questions in situations where you can learn. You have the tools around you to grow into who you are meant to be. Be confident that there is only one you. You are unique, one of a kind, no one else on earth can do, think, breathe, or show up like you. Use who you are today to become who you were meant to be.

I'm not perfect, and I have made more embarrassing mistakes than words in this book. We can choose to use those mistakes as guide posts and building blocks to live a life with greater intention rather than looking at those as painful memories. Let those times serve you to become the best, most intention-filled person you can be. You've got it all.

YOUR INTENTION EXERCISE:

1. Consider how you can *wake up* and be better prepared for your day. Where are you falling short? What behaviors do you need to change or add to your routine to be more present for your commitments?
2. What steps do you need to take to build your community? Who can you reach out to today to lay the foundation for your personal Board of Directors? Make a list of anyone you consider a sponsor. Make a second list of individuals you want to add to your sponsor list and consider what you might do to build that relationship. Take action!
3. Quickly name three goals you have for this year. Jot them down. How might you find your way to the finish line before the year is up?
4. Look at your calendar for the month. Do you have a commitment on the calendar that you chose to do but really don't have the time? Is it something you could

eliminate and use the space in your day in a better way? Where do you believe you need to set more boundaries? Write these down on a Post-it Note and hang it from the bottom of your computer screen, or put it in a place where it can remind you of this commitment to yourself and your schedule.

5. Believe in yourself more than you believe in your most impressive friend. Jot down three things you have in your life that you are truly grateful for. Bonus points if you can do this each day inside today's date in your planner. Feel stuck? Start with the weather, your favorite shoes, a hot coffee… make it simple and grow from there.

You got this, let's go!

TOP 4 TAKEAWAYS:

1. **Clarity:** Having intentions brings clarity to your life by helping you establish clear goals and objectives. When you know what you want to achieve and have a specific intention behind it, you are more likely to stay focused and make decisions that align with your goals.

2. **Motivation:** Intention provides a sense of purpose and motivation. When you have a clear intention for what you want to achieve, it becomes easier to stay motivated, especially during challenging times. Intentions act as a driving force that helps you overcome obstacles and setbacks, keeping you on track toward your goals.

3. **Alignment:** Intention ensures your actions and choices align with your values and beliefs. It helps you stay true to yourself and make decisions that align with your long-term objectives. By having intention, you ensure that you

are living a life that is true to who you are, which leads to a greater sense of fulfillment and happiness.

4. **Productivity:** Having intention in your life helps you become more productive as it gives you a clear direction and purpose. It prevents you from wasting time and energy on activities or goals that do not align with what you truly desire. When you have intention, you can prioritize and focus on tasks that are meaningful and contribute to your overall goals, leading to increased productivity and success.

CHAPTER 3

Improve Discipline

―――――

My middle school track uniform was green mesh shorts, a bright yellow T-shirt, and white Nike socks pulled halfway up my calves. I had a long blonde ponytail and enjoyed every minute of getting faster and competing at the meets. I went to the State meet in eighth grade and placed sixth in the mile. At the age of thirteen, I began to see the results of my disciplined practice. Our coaches made it easy for us: just show up after school each day and do what they say!

As we grow older and enter adulthood, those coaches leave our daily practice, and we must fend for ourselves. Our bosses might create deadlines and sales goals, but we are on our own to organize our day in a way we will stay productive and meet our goals. It ain't easy! Distractions abound, and *the grind* sets in.

Long gone are the days of lacing up my hand-me-down track shoes and yellow T-shirt to follow the coaches' plans. I have a to-do list to finish a plan designed on my own. In these moments, the discipline I learned in those early days kicks in. Small, consistent efforts over time produce results, even when a sixth-place ribbon is your ultimate prize.

After college, I found myself floundering. I was living in Chicago, finding myself in a similar situation to the one I had survived when I entered college—small fish, big pond. I had a great starter job working for the Chicago Bulls in ticket sales with a clear goal: make sales, but it was a boring task, making countless calls. I was dying in my dream job, shrinking into the roller chair in my tiny cube, feeling uninspired and worried. Was I mediocre? Did I pick the right career? I'd watch TV at night for three hours in the brownstone I shared with three roommates, head to my IKEA bed to sleep for eight hours, and commute to work again the next day. I was living the dream in a big city in what many considered the prime years of my life, but in reality, my life was monotonous.

A girl I worked with, Abby, ran the Disney Marathon. I watched her work diligently at her training, and she talked to us about her long runs during our lunch hour. I remembered my days of training and knew that was the kind of goal I needed to get back to a clear, goal-directed mind. I needed a training program to keep me disciplined. I needed a coach.

I used the printer at work to spit out Hal Higdon's half marathon training program, and I got to work. I ran each night around the streets of Chicago with my tiny MP3 player on my arm and a watch calculating my mileage on my wrist. The steady drum beat and assignment to run at night kept me out of trouble. Less partying, more discipline. I ran the Louisville Half Marathon that spring after training all winter in Chicago.

My family came down to watch me run and cheered me on, just like when I competed in the eighth-grade Illinois State Championship.

Years passed between races, but the discipline of committing to exercise stayed with me. When life at work was a bore, I'd look forward to a group fitness class at my gym or a run on the lakefront.

In the back of my head, I heard the whisper, marathon, but put it off until after the birth of my third child. When I told my dad (who was at that half marathon in Louisville all those years ago) that I'd signed up for the race, he responded, "I always knew you'd do it." Sometimes, the people around you can identify your goals before they become clear to you.

I confirmed my goal, and it was time to get training. My husband was a true partner in this goal, helping me to find the right app to track my runs, doing research on hydration and energy, ensuring I had the right shoes, and taking over watching the kids on the long run days.

I'd finish my runs and send him a picture with my time. I was getting faster and more comfortable. Mostly, I enjoyed it. A goal I had put off for twenty-five years was in motion. I had the momentum, I had the support, and I had the discipline to remain committed to my goal.

I used an app to supply my training and felt the fulfillment of a green check mark when I completed my run. I had accountability in the form of an app on my iPhone identified by a tiny blue square.

The September race day arrived, and I was ready. My sideline cheerleaders included my dad, my oldest son Magnus, and my husband. Each person at that race held a key to my completion of the race: my dad as the reminder of how far I'd come, my son as my inspiration, and my husband who had helped me to remain disciplined in my goal.

When I finished the race, I certainly felt exhausted, but I also felt a tremendous sense of accomplishment and pride in myself. I knew I could do anything I set my mind to, and this was just another example of working hard to accomplish a goal and remaining disciplined.

I don't believe in one and done. I think we have to keep pushing ourselves to do more to achieve personal growth. Marathon training was my ultimate test of discipline. The only person who could do the work was me.

A combination of the tiny voice inside, a support system, and an interest in achieving a new goal helped me to stay the course.

HOW YOU CAN APPLY DISCIPLINE TO ACHIEVE YOUR GOALS

Employ the tools that are available to you to hold you accountable. Have someone in your corner to cheer you on, support you, and not let you off the hook. Call your shot, tell your support circle, and do not let yourself down. A person with high self-confidence has high self-trust. Build a reputation with yourself that you do the things you say you are going to do. Each day, you are out there running, chasing, working, and doing the next right thing, your future self is thanking you endlessly for the discipline you are showing today.

Noel Mirhadi, who was with United Talent Agency when I interviewed her on the *Leadership is Female* Podcast, is now with Oak View Group and has employed discipline to excel in her career. Noel focuses on booking artists into all venue types, including performing arts centers, clubs, theaters, amphitheaters, and festivals. Noel attended college in Syracuse, moved to New York, started as a receptionist, and is now in Los Angeles working in her dream role. I describe her ability to achieve this in two words: laser focus.

She credits her success to staying true to her key interest: music. She started playing the cello in fourth grade, creating a pathway for her career as a music talent agent to book live concert events.

Noel said, "I chose the cello. I can't really explain it. It drew me in. So, I studied performance in college and was interested in continuing my music but also chose an industry track to study the business side of the music industry while maintaining a base in my own performance, which I love."[1]

Running right alongside her laser focus is discipline. It took discipline to stay the course. I think Noel's key life hack here is her tremendous interest in music. The lift to stay disciplined was lighter because she loves to practice.

You might look at Noel and think, easy for her! She found her passion and stuck with it; it came naturally. However, think about Noel's favorite quote by former YouTube CEO Susan Wojcicki, given during her John Hopkins University Commencement Speech. "Rarely are opportunities presented to you in a perfect way. In a nice little box with a yellow bow on top. 'Here, open it, it's perfect. You'll love it.' Opportunities— the good ones—are messy, confusing, and hard to recognize. They're risky. They challenge you."[2]

Noel might be able to reflect and present a nicely packaged summary of her career, but at its core, it is her discipline to stay committed to marrying both her goals and her passions. She's equally excited about the challenge and the opportunity as she is about the work it will take her to reach her goal.

Take notice of what you do when you have the freedom to choose. Are you cooking, creating content for social media, editing videos, writing, practicing your cello, or going on long runs? What are you interested in? How can you build a career around that interest and create the disciple to stay the course, excel more easily, and dare I say, have fun?

Zaileen Janmohamed is a passionate leader with a wealth of holistic experience on the brand, agency, and property sides of the sports marketing business. As the former United States Olympic and Paralympic's head of partnership development and innovation and now president and CEO of the Bay Area Host Committee, Zaileen works at the intersection of sales, partner management, and community activation.

Zaileen has two sons, a husband, and a busy career. She advises us to "Get organized and figure out the logistics of your whole life, including career, family, and friends.

Ask for help and communicate. There is only stress in the ambiguity."[3]

If you create a clear plan and integrate others, you'll have a better chance of staying committed to the work. Operating in a state of disciple helps you to achieve successful, disciplined repetition, and train your brain to work in this mindset.

She acknowledges there will be low times in life when we lack discipline. When that happens, get the help you need to bring you through to the other side and find the silver lining in the tough experiences. Let the hard times happen for us, not to us.

"You can be a high achiever and still have a low-key mindset to life,"[4] Zaileen said. Her trick? Laugh to decompress!

THE RESEARCH BEHIND THE BENEFIT OF APPLYING DISCIPLINE TO YOUR LIFE

In her TEDx Talk, "The Power of Loving Discipline," Elizabeth Judith explores the toxic love-hate relationship many of us have with self-discipline. She says, "Self-discipline is a powerful tool for achieving success, but it can be a source of stress and shame if not managed properly. Developing a healthy relationship with self-discipline is essential to our well-being. By embracing discipline as an expression of self-love, we cultivate a positive relationship with the Self that enables us to live to our full potential."[5]

Elizabeth cautions employing discipline as a people-pleasing tool; one that would pursue results to get the external validation to make you feel you are finally enough.

She cautions bullying yourself into action. Check-in on how you are feeling, and she lays out ways to do so, including the mantra, "Discipline will give you a beautiful life."[6]

With this mantra, she created the Loving Discipline Method that goes deeper than external results. It could be a feeling and a state of being. It encourages you to be a student on a journey to love and grow. When we live from our highest self and potential, we naturally reach the unique positive impact we came here to make, and we feel fantastic when we are doing it.

It takes being a devoted student to attend class every day ready to learn. But the fixed mindset can get in the way. Through Dr. Carol Dweck's research, she defines fixed vs growth mindset, and I think it's worth a reminder to serve as a gut check for you.

She states, "Believing that your qualities are carved in stone—the fixed mindset—creates an urgency to prove yourself over and over. If you have only a certain amount of intelligence, a certain personality, and a certain moral character-well, then you'd better prove that you have a healthy dose of them. It simply wouldn't do to look or feel deficient in the most basic characteristics."[7] With a fixed mindset, we will shy away from challenges that might allow us to grow and instead dedicate our time and energy toward protecting our ego and not exposing our feelings of lack.

In contrast, the growth mindset tells us that our abilities and talents can grow and develop. We can learn whatever we need to achieve whatever we want! Where we are now is simply a jumping-off point. Challenges and failures are simply an opportunity to grow.

An amazing gap exists between where we are and where we want to be. However, this is an opportunity. The growth mindset of being a devoted student is all about believing and tapping into our infinite potential, knowing, understanding, and evolving ourselves from a place of curiosity.

Cultivating curiosity toward self requires courage. Shame, a derisive of a fixed mindset, destroys our curiosity. Our conditioning tells us to criticize ourselves which causes damage to our brains, our psychological well-being, and our relationships with self. Shame will never give us the life of our dreams.

The only way to get to your goals is through self-discipline. I found that practicing discipline through dedicated training, like running a race, bled over into other areas of my life.

Noel found discipline by pursuing a linear path. She explored and grew her life through her passion for music. She has hobbies, a career, and a social life inside of something she loves.

Ask yourself what you love and if it's possible to create a career around that topic. Showing up every day to earn for yourself and your family is a much lighter lift when it's filled with enjoyment.

As Elizabeth stated, use your curiosity in a disciplined manner. You should live life, and a beautiful life exists where we continuously challenge our potential.

Shift your mindset around discipline. It is not a punishment but a growth opportunity.

EXERCISE: LET'S FIND WAYS TO IMPROVE YOUR SELF-DISCIPLINE:

1. Take notice of the things you enjoy doing when you have the freedom to choose. What are they?
2. Have you accomplished a goal lately? If so, reflect on how you did it. If you fell short, reflect on why.
3. What challenges have you loved taking on? What are you excited about?
4. List all your excuses for not sticking to your last goal. Which of these can you overcome and how?
5. How can you make time to do more of what you enjoy? Where will these enjoyable pursuits fit into your schedule?

If you've failed at a goal, stop beating yourself up. Forgive yourself and decide to move on. Maybe this goal no longer serves you. That's ok. We evolve! Letting it go makes space for something new. To grow your self-discipline, start by working toward a goal you enjoy. This will not only build your confidence for your next pursuit, but it will give you a successful repetition of discipline. Confidence grows when you keep the promises you make to yourself.

TOP FOUR TAKEAWAYS:

1. **Achieving goals:** Self-discipline will help you focus and stay committed to your goals. The longer you can stay the path, the greater your chance of success. Remain disciplined, and you will be able to resist and repel distractions; your discipline will put up a wall and block out anything that attempts to divert you from your goal. Why set goals? Simply because your accomplishments will lead to a greater sense of fulfillment in life. That feels good.

2. **Improved productivity:** When you have self-discipline, you develop effective habits and routines that enhance your productivity. You'll begin to prioritize important tasks, manage your time more efficiently, and avoid procrastination. Increased efficiency and output in both your personal and professional life will give you a beautiful feeling: a sense of accomplishment!

3. **Enhanced self-control:** Improved discipline strengthens your ability to control your impulses. You'll make better decisions, resist temptations, and overcome bad habits. Through continuous work on self-control, you can avoid impulsive actions that can negatively impact your health, relationships, and work.

4. **Increased resilience:** Self-discipline builds resilience, enabling you to bounce back from setbacks and persevere during challenging times. It helps you maintain a positive mindset because you have a routine to fall back on. Discipline will help you to stay motivated! You will develop the mental strength necessary to overcome obstacles and grow from adversity instead of letting it hold you back.

CHAPTER 4

Get Uncomfortable

―――

"Get comfortable being uncomfortable." I was in my mid-twenties when I first heard this quote. Flashes of sweaty palms, dread, and constant butterflies were the only emotions I could consider when I thought about being uncomfortable. "No thanks," would be my reply. Turns out that real growth comes from a place of discomfort. When I began to wrap my mind around what these moments of discomfort could do *for* me rather than do *to* me, I really saw personal growth.

Picking up the phone to call a stranger and asking for a sale made my stomach turn over. We had a sales system at the Chicago Bulls that would literally populate a call list for us every morning. I'd walk into my tiny cubicle, log into to the computer, and a small gray box would pop up on the screen with my day's work. You grow a business by selling things and cold calls and cold outreach are still key players in this game.

Eighty calls. Eighty calls a day! As a twenty-one-year-old straight out of college with a huge phobia of talking to people, I didn't know this would be my worst nightmare. How could

I have selected a job with this task as the required daily work? What was I thinking?

My goal was to work in sports. Ever since I was a kid, sports have helped me get along in life. I enjoyed life in my small town by playing sports at home with my brothers and became part of a community on my local club soccer team.

I didn't know the *in* to the sports industry for most people was taking a job in ticket sales. This meant my primary role was making calls to people on a lead list and asking them to buy season tickets or determining if they had an interest in creating a group of twenty-five or more to get a discount on game tickets.

I turned down a full-time salary job in the sexy advertising industry in Chicago to take this full-time nine-dollar-an-hour internship. Each week, two over-performing interns had the opportunity to earn extra money. The first way was to win one of two contests: make the most calls or make the most sales. The second was to earn commission on our sales after hitting a minimum revenue number. The caveat to the commission was our sales number reset every week!

At the start of the internship, we entered sales training. I sat in a fancy conference room inside the United Center with my black Express blazer, feeling like I'd made it. We read scripts, talked rebuttals, and learned how to ask for the sale.

Nearing the end of day two, I learned we'd take turns practicing our new scripts in a role-playing exercise at the head of the room, one-on-one in front of all our classmates.

This is where the saying entered my life: "Get comfortable being uncomfortable."

When it was my turn, my cheeks were hot with embarrassment before I even stuttered a word. What was that canned rebuttable we had practiced again? Was I saying the right thing? I made it to the end of the call, and my partner said, "I don't have enough money!" And simply hung up.

Half-hearted applause filled the room, and I returned to my seat. I felt damp from all that nervous sweating, but I was still breathing.

I went home that night and thought about my commitment. I took this job, signed up for this role, and ultimately won this spot to do this *terrible* job among a thousand applications. I had said "yes," and with that commitment, I knew I couldn't quit.

I made it through training alive. I didn't die of embarrassment or discomfort. I determined I could do this.

I made thousands of uncomfortable phone calls throughout my time with the Bulls. I even sold some tickets. On the weeks when I knew I couldn't place first in sales, I did my best to beat out a guy named Bobby for the most calls and earn an extra one hundred dollars.

We had a sales leaderboard with the name of every intern displaying their sales figures in two categories: group sales and season tickets. We sold group sales tickets for one game to a group of more than twenty-five people. We sold season tickets as one or more seats to one person or business for the entire season. I finished my internship in first place in group sales. I was at the top of the leaderboard. I grew from sweating through my suit coat making a single call to first place in one of two sales categories. I can explain my experience in this job in one word: growth.

I grew from a shy-but-ready-to-take-on-the-world twenty-one-year-old into a whopping twenty-two-year-old who was a leader in sales, all in nine months.

I got comfortable being uncomfortable. I knew discomfort was a necessary ingredient in growth. If I wanted to do more, to be more, I had to stretch myself beyond the norm and operate in a circle of newness that was not always so cushy and fun.

I pushed myself to do that, and I did it in a few ways.

The first was recognizing my *Why*. In this instance, it was because of my commitment to the job, my commitment to start my career, and my commitment to fulfill a dream from when I was a child.

My *Why* was commitment. Stick and commit.

When faced with the reality that you need to operate in an uncomfortable place, consider what you committed to get there. What is your *Why*? Money, growth, passion, achievement, or because you don't have another damn choice?

Identify your *why* and operate with that vision.

A funny thing happens when you are human. You grow accustomed to things. The action that once made your deodorant fail now comes second nature.

Cold calls previously dialed with trembling fingers you now complete without a second thought.

Conversations with strangers become exciting ones of discovery rather than a thumping heartbeat and foggy mind.

We can push into a level of discomfort and must live there for a while, but then our body gives us the ultimate break. We get used to it. It becomes a function of our operation and success. Activate your willpower to push through the pain because on the other side is growth. And with this growth comes a newfound confidence.

Since my early days, this lesson has accompanied me with every new task, job, and goal I encounter since recognizing discomfort equals growth.

Every time I do something new, *boom*, there it is. Sweaty palms are back, heart thumping, with my brain telling me, "Just run the other way, Emily, and you can go back to that nice place of comfort!"

At this point, I ask myself, *Who are you today, and who do you want to be?* That woman does not shy away from discomfort because she wants to grow. I want to lead. I want to speak. I want to share my thoughts.

To do that, I need to speak up, show up, and do my best work. That effort requires, well, effort. Pushing beyond the discomfort to do the thing you set out to accomplish.

In college, I took a speech class. Glossophobia, or fear of public speaking, is a very common phobia and one that is believed to affect up to 75 percent of the population.[1] In our class inside the Armory at the University of Illinois, that stat was nearly one hundred percent, and I was convinced the only classmates not affected were those who simply didn't care.

I'd prepare my speech, create my notecards, and give a presentation that was, on average, more than two minutes longer than the time they gave me to deliver it. I rambled, paraphrased, and was indirect. I don't even think I got an *A* in that class, and they always marketed speech communications as an easy class for athletes.

Years later, I speak on stage in front of hundreds of people. It was not easy to get here. A combination of willpower and envisioning the type of woman I wanted to become mixed with practice, feedback, and endless trial and error. What drove me was my vision of the woman I wanted to become. She wasn't in the back of the room but on stage with a set of work experiences, wisdom, stories, and helpful notes to share with an audience.

WHY YOU SHOULD APPLY DISCOMFORT AND HOW TO MANAGE IT

Did you know putting yourself in unfamiliar situations triggers your brain to release dopamine? Dopamine is the *make-you-happy* chemical. It seems counterintuitive, right? Well, here is the real kicker: the unique dopamine-releasing area of your brain activates only when you see or experience something completely new.

A *Forbes* article, "Why Feeling Uncomfortable Is the Key to Success" by Sujan Patel, offers four steps to help you through the discomfort so you can experience the gain, dopamine hit, and all:

1. **Clear your mind.** This works differently for everyone, but the most common strategies include taking a walk to decompress and move through your discomfort, doing a brain dump by writing all your ideas out on paper, or talking about the discomfort with another person.
2. **Identify the source.** The source may be clear, but can you identify why you are feeling the way you are? What about the situation triggers the discomfort? Name the origin, legitimize it, and take back your power.
3. **Reflect.** When was a time you were uncomfortable and survived? Celebrate your wins and remind yourself of the growth that came from a previous situation where you were not sure if you would succeed. Use that example to explain to yourself how you can persevere through the next challenge.
4. **Take the plunge.** If you feel uncomfortable, you are on the right track. Therefore, take the first step![2]

Patel finishes with this hard hitter, "Ultimately, you have to find the courage, awareness, and undressing that allow you to see problems and hurdles for what they really are: opportunities to grow and learn."[3]

REAL-LIFE EXAMPLES

Courtney Rice, VP at RevelXP, an elite fan experiences company in the sports and entertainment industry that creates unforgettable game day hospitality for their clients, fans, and brands, had to get very uncomfortable to make progress in her career. Courtney started working in a similar role to mine at the Bulls, just three hours south down Highway I-65, at the Indiana Pacers.

Her goal was to get into some type of work inside the pro sports industry after playing D1 soccer at Illinois State. Courtney said, "Playing college sports prepared me immensely for going into sales in general because I was ready for the *Nos* and the hard conversations."[4]

Despite this preparation, Courtney said during her first month in her role with the Pacers, she really questioned if she should be doing it. "I felt like an imposter. I didn't think I'd be good at sales. Cold calling scared me, but I dug deep, pushed myself to get uncomfortable, and figured out what worked best for me in the sales world."[5]

She found her style and what it took to make her successful: making better, fewer calls. She did this by doubling down on her requests for referrals. She'd speak with fewer people who didn't want to talk to her and become more efficient with a higher level of success.

She got creative in her process by finding a way to sell that fit her personality and style. When she considered how she landed the job in the first place, she connected the dots to understand they awarded her an internship because of the people she spoke to on campus while networking.

Courtney had defined her end goal to work in the sports industry during college. To get there she had to meet people to find a job. She did that on campus in the city in which she wanted to work. From there, she received a job offer that was not quite perfect: an internship in ticket sales where the daily task, sales, and cold calls, made her immensely uncomfortable.

Courtney has lived her life by getting out of her comfort zone and living in discomfort. Through reflection, she discovered what she was good at: networking. She deployed this skill during her uncomfortable moments to forge a new way of doing the job. One that worked for her but still completed the task.

Learning and finding a way to master a new skill improved Courtney's confidence. She grew and expanded her comfort zone.

You can, too.

Embrace the moments of discomfort and imagine what it will feel like for you when you are on the other side. You have changed. You have expanded. You have grown. You are capable of so much more when you dig deep and keep showing up for yourself and the hard stuff.

Envision who you will be and what you can do on the other side. This is the thought pattern that will motivate you to show up for the discomfort every day. It might feel gradual, but eventually, the discomfort will ease. You'll feel at ease in the task that once felt like lifting an elephant. This, my friend, is growth, and it's the best feeling in the world.

In Bill Eckstrom's TEDXUniversity of Nevada titled, "Why Comfort Will Ruin your Life," he discussed how getting fired from his executive job created the biggest amount of discomfort he had ever felt. The discomforting departure from his ordered, routine life in the corporate world forever changed him for the better.

Bill says, "What makes you comfortable can ruin you, and only in a state of discomfort can you continually grow."[6]

Following his firing and with some help from his PhD friends, Bill worked to create a concept called The Growth Rings to illustrate and apply the science of discomfort and growth. They represent living environments that promote or hinder growth, equating your place of work to your fishbowl.[7]

Did you know the size of a fishbowl determines the size of the fish? It's the same for you. The environments in which you work, live, and play dictate your growth.[8]

According to Bill, these are The Growth Rings:

- **Chaos.** An environment of little to no control where high turmoil halts growth.
- **Complexity.** An unpredictable environment where outcomes are unknown.
- **Order.** A comfortable environment that leads to a predictable outcome.
- **Stagnation.** A low performing or negative growth environment.[9]

You can learn how empowering it is to choose discomfort and, when appropriate, choose complexity over order.

Yes, the order and stagnation phases of the ring sound well comfortable! Cozy, like the perfect Lazy Boy chair in front of a warm fireplace. Your favorite Starbucks in hand and some warm socks. The fuzzy blanket you received as a birthday gift from your grandmother draped over your legs.

As you are dreaming, dozing by the fire, something lights in your brain. A tiny flicker of a reminder that choosing complexity over order is the only environment where sustained or exponential growth can occur.

It's here we kick off that blanket and exchange those warm socks for your best pair of get-stuff-done shoes and leave that fire to go take on the world.

Your willpower is that tiny flicker in your brain. It can break through your comfort and remind you that you are made for more. Listen to that tiny voice and feel that tiny flame. Let it push you up to go after what you want. It is the push through to action where your confidence will grow.

If you are wondering how exactly to feel that flicker, there are three triggers that Bill describes in his Growth Ring Model:

1. Someone forced it upon you. When this happens, you have no choice, like someone firing you. When this happens, how much you grow depends on how you respond to it.
2. Someone can help you get there. This is the role of parents, teachers, coaches, and bosses. Left on their own, people will consciously or subconsciously select the comfort of order. People need a push into complexity to continue growing. This is where you make critical developmental decisions.
3. Trigger it yourself. If you are not lucky enough to live and work in a robust high-growth environment, you must trigger it yourself.[10]

In the second scenario, someone can help you get there, and someone can also get you out. Your parents, your spouse, and your friend who might ask you why you are so uncomfortable and what they can do to help make you happy again. While well-intentioned, what they are actually doing is stifling your development. Stay strong in your resolve to get yourself to the next level.

Eckstrom says, "It's not the complexity triggering individuals or events you should fear the most, but it's your own willingness to accept or seek discomfort that will dictate the growth of not just you, but our entire world."[11]

Both Courtney and I accepted and opted into the discomfort. We chose to stay. We chose to learn. We chose to grow into the women we are today.

Choosing uncomfortable situations with wavering confidence at the start is the exact behavior you need to change your attitude to one with greater confidence. This choice to show up in discomfort every day helped Courtney and me become the more confident, talk-to-anyone, cold-calling, sales-making, ladder-climbing women we are today because we chose discomfort.

Make yourself uncomfortable today, and your future self will reap the rewards.

HOW TO APPLY DISCOMFORT TO YOUR ADVANTAGE

Here is an exercise for you to keep close to your chest any time your nerves threaten to interrupt your progress.

Think of a goal you have that's scary, one that makes the butterflies in your stomach feel more like bats. Ask yourself why that's your goal. Why do you even want to do this task or take on this new, challenging goal? This answer is what drives you to get it done. Remember Chapter 1, "Find Your *Why*?" This is when the application gets practical.

Name that *Why* and keep it close. Your *Why* is the only thing that can help ease the pain of your discomfort because on the other side of the nerves you are feeling is personal growth.

TOP FOUR TAKEAWAYS:

1. **Growth and learning:** Being uncomfortable forces you to confront challenges and learn new skills to overcome them. When we live in a constant state of comfort, it

means we are sticking to what we already know and limiting our growth in all areas of our lives. Embrace discomfort, charge at it with open arms, and allow yourself to learn, adapt, and improve yourself, ultimately leading to greater success.

2. **Resilience and adaptability:** Success always requires you to be resilient and adaptable in the face of uncertainty. Being uncomfortable helps to build your resilience when it forces you to navigate challenging situations and bounce back from setbacks.

3. **Overcoming limiting beliefs and fears:** Discomfort challenges you to confront your limiting beliefs and fears, pushing you to step outside your comfort zone. Don't hold yourself back because of self-doubt or fear of failure. You can push past your fears to realize your full potential.

4. **Innovation and creativity:** Discomfort can be a catalyst for innovation and creativity. It forces you to think outside the box and come up with unconventional solutions. Tackle difficult problems head-on, and you will tap into your creative abilities, leading to innovative ideas and successful outcomes. With competence comes confidence.

CHAPTER 5

Become Curious

———

When I got the call to be GM of a Minor League Baseball team, I probably knew about fifty percent of what it took to get the job done. The rest I was certain I would figure out. Could I ask about the rest? Should I look cool and pretend I knew? Should I really lean in on the fifty-year-old quip, "fake it until you make it"? On my first day of work, I was swimming in inspirational quote soup wondering what my approach would be to management and to all the areas I was uncertain about how to tackle.

I went with "fake it until you make it" and thought I could observe my way to success. I worked mostly in the areas I already knew and listened hard on league calls to learn what I didn't. I still had a gaping hole in the knowledge required to do the job.

I showed up to the press conference announcing my position to the media with notes of gratitude for the job. They invited my family to be photographed with me and presented me with a jersey with my name on the back. With the TV cameras rolling, I fielded more questions about what food the ballpark would serve rather than any hard-hitting questions about the stability of the business or the success of the team.

Working in an atmosphere of adrenaline and fright, I wondered about the next time someone would ask me something I didn't know. It felt like divine intervention when a *Harvard Business Review* showed up in my office on my desk with a cover story entitled "The Business Case for Curiosity" with a tagline of "Research Shows that It Leads to Higher-Performing, more-Adaptable Firms."[1] Here it was, my permission slip to ask all the questions.

Harvard Business School's Francesca Gino elaborated on the benefits of and common barriers to curiosity in the workplace and offered five strategies for bolstering it, "Although leaders might *say* they value inquisitive minds, in reality, most stifle curiosity, fearing it will increase risk and inefficiency. Leaders should hire for curiosity, model inquisitiveness, emphasize learning goals, let workers explore and broaden their interests, and have 'Why? 'What if…?' and 'How might we…?' days. Doing so will help their organizations adapt to uncertain market conditions and external pressures and boost the business's success."[2]

Here it was, the key to success. Curiosity. I could ask a damn question.

I remember entering my boss's cluttered office for our weekly meeting. With my hands full, along with the *Harvard Business Review,* I couldn't find room for my laptop computer or assortment of drinks on his paper-filled desk. I placed it in the chair next to me for our one-on-one and slowly unloaded my bounty, mostly to the floor, to begin our meeting.

He wanted to know how the first few months had gone. Grateful for his curiosity, I told him my plan was to observe. We were in season when I arrived, and I didn't want to derail any year-long plans in motion but still govern the business in a way only I could do. When it came to the business of baseball, I watched and listened, seeking out the key players and successful repeatable moments, and asked the staff for excellence.

An area that was new to me involved all the guys downstairs in the clubhouse, the players, the managers, the clubbies, and the relationship with our major league club. I was a fish out of water. I knew how to treat people and had formed wonderful relationships by simply giving a damn about them but streamlining business operations would require me to digest a big slice of humble pie. I'd have to ask a lot more questions instead of pretending I knew what I was doing.

When I started the role, my boss had told me, "Clubhouse management is only ten percent of your job, and I can do it with my eyes closed, so you'll learn quickly." The difference? He had twenty years of experience in that area of the business. I was a novice.

I didn't want to look like I didn't know what I was doing or like it was hard, so I leaned on the skills I had, including relationship building, but remained blind to how to make a real impact because I didn't really understand how. I had been silent in any effort to ask the question, "How can I help?" because I didn't already have the answer.

...until I walked into the office with the *Harvard Business Review.*

I held up the magazine and gave the summary. Curiosity would help our business. Asking questions would lead to discovering outcomes and efficiencies we might not yet be aware of. This was 2018, long before curiosity became an acceptable business term shared among leadership teams. *Curiosity* was a word I could use like body armor. I could hide behind my lack of knowledge in a certain area and pose any question I had as a curiosity to enhance the business.

No one said I had to know it all. No one said I couldn't ask questions. In fact, people love to give advice and solve your problems. It can stroke their egos.

We discussed the article, he agreed, and I was off to the races. The magazine sat in my office for nearly four years. It would collect dust in between references, but it was always there. It was my armor. It would be difficult to count the times I used that article as a tool for the people I managed. I gave them permission to get curious. Permission to ask questions they did not know the answers to. We could work together to make the business stronger.

When I applied this tool to the clubhouse, I became a damn good manager. Why did we do things the same way as before? Was there an opportunity for improvement?

I called and got quotes from new vendors, interviewed other team's GMs to see how they did it, created new tracking systems, and spent more time with the team in the clubhouse talking to the manager and players. I asked them hard questions like, "What could we do better?" "What do you need?" The information I gathered was powerful.

I didn't know what I was doing when I started, but the more time I spent in the clubhouse asking questions and searching for new answers, the more efficient our business became. Things got better, from ordering uniforms to feeding the players, to travel and flights, and our dialed-in uniform schedule. Relationships improved, and Reno became one of the best places to manage a team or visit to play.

How can you know the answer to a problem you've never encountered? The fact is, you can't. Get curious, phone a friend, or ask a colleague or someone with more experience than you who is doing the same thing. When did we allow our egos to stop us from admitting when we didn't know the answer? Thank you, *Harvard Business Review,* for hitting a home run on normalizing curiosity.

Mallory LePage, Director of Global Partnerships for the Milwaukee Bucks, applied the concept of curiosity to propel herself into a top position with a leading NBA team. She didn't know much about sales or that it would ultimately lead her to the position she wanted with a sports team. She just trusted that if she got curious, one day she'd make it to the role she coveted, which, early in her career, was simply a role at the top.

Early in her advertising sales days, her curiosity was two-fold. Client-side, she asked lots of questions about their business to find the best solution. Internally, she collaborated with her boss to learn the tricks of the trade. She asked questions like, "How many calls should I make?" "How do I prepare the best pitch?" "What sales follow-up works best?" and "What types of clients are most likely to buy?" All these lead to her growth.

Ultimately, as Mallory put it, the road she took, "Helped teach me about adversity, being independent, being self-reliant, being self-motivated, and just having really tough jobs along the way. My worst job was my best job, selling gas station radio because ultimately, they hired me under the premise that if I can sell gas station radio, I can sell NBA basketball." [3]

On her sales journey, she learned that you must get curious with your customers. You might have objectives you want to meet, but you must be patient and hear them out. You must listen to what the client wants and fit their objectives into your offerings. Curiosity is a thread that runs through the entire sales process.

* * *

At the end of 2018, a mentorship program launched in Minor League Baseball. I was curious. I wondered what it would look like for me to mentor a woman early in her career from a different city who worked for another team. I was lucky enough, after filling out the interest survey, to pair up with a girl named Rachael.

She was a diligent worker and a former athlete, and she worked for a Double-A team that asked its employees to do it all. Lucky for them, Rachael was up for anything and never shied away from effort. Instead of saying, "I don't know how to do that," and rejecting the task, Rachael got curious to figure it out and then used what she learned to do it with excellence.

Rachael's title was Community Relations Manager, but in addition to community events to bolster the team's involvement in enriching the lives of those in her city of Midland, she was also responsible for writing press releases, public relations work on social media platforms, and running the suite level on game day. For a new college grad, she was well beyond her scope of knowledge and was not afraid to ask questions. That curiosity came easy. Interpersonal curiosity brought her to a new level.

Her curiosity has had an enormous benefit on her people skills in the fast-paced, high-stress event environment. Rachael said, "My biggest growth area has come from having patience in working with different types of people. I used to be bad at my reactions. I have really had to learn how to stay curious about people rather than getting mad. I take a breath, don't respond right away, and think about what might have caused them to do what they did. Keeping a mindset of curiosity has tremendously helped when dealing with difficult people." [4]

Rachael excelled in Minor League Baseball and really shined in her role in the community. Involvement with the sport she loved, volleyball, pulled her in that direction, and she took a coaching role. Working in baseball all day and coaching in her free time, she got curious about what her life would look like with a career change. She started asking questions, and the answer revealed itself with a job offer: become a teacher and a full-time volleyball coach.

Curiosity works everywhere in your life, from clients to interpersonal skills to getting curious about a new career. Use the lens of curiosity to help you through life's big challenges.

Curiosity didn't kill the cat. Curiosity revived the cat.

YOUR CURIOSITY REFLECTION:
- Do you wonder how to foster a more curious environment? Do you feel you need to get or give permission to be more curious from your family or in your workplace?
- What is one topic or activity you can get curious about today?
- What is one thing you usually take for granted that you want to ask about? Ask some "why questions" today.
- "What will happen if?" I can get nervous about a post, an email, a call, or a new challenge, but somehow, the whole effort softens if I approach it from a curious angle rather than one of high stakes. Try this approach and watch your work become less stressful, your conversations richer, and your efforts have more ease.

TOP FOUR TAKEAWAYS:
The *Harvard Business Review* article that changed my attitude around "faking it until I make it" to one as a fundamentally

curious leader and employee states the following benefits of curiosity:

1. If you are curious, you will make fewer decision-making errors because we are less likely to fall victim to confirmation bias.
2. If your employees are curious, your company can have more innovation and better job performance.
3. If your company is curious, you can experience fewer defensive reactions, less aggressive reactions to challenges, and more empathy.
4. Curious employees are more open in their communication and perform better as a team. [5]

PART II:

MINDSET

CHAPTER 6

Develop Consistency

——

I left my routine of the daily work hustle in early 2022. I did the same thing nearly every day for over three years: wake up, write out my day, shower and dress, get the kids up and ready, make lunches and breakfast with a protein shake for me, coffee, and kiss my husband goodbye. Then, I'd drop off the kids, get to work, hustle until lunch, work out, and get back to meetings, calls, and decisions until 5:30 p.m. (unless there was a game). Afterward, I'd pick up the kids, arrive home, make dinner, clean up after the meal, and put the kids to bed.

When I left my job as GM, I departed from an identity, a leadership role, and a routine I had grown accustomed to. I had to figure out a new normal. I was working for myself in a home office with no one around but my computer and my dogs. The dogs would ask me for a walk. I'd do it. Laundry would call my name. I'll just put in a load. Oh, here's my Peloton. It's time for a workout. Now shower… in the middle of the morning. Then I'd notice dirty counters and clean them. Do we have anything for dinner? I'll pick something up. The distraction of email and online shopping crept in. I'd look to post on Instagram about my business and instead lose myself in a sea of other people's news. Oh, a text from my husband. I'd answer it. Eventually, I'd accomplish a task on the list for the day, but everything I did was free-floating and unplanned. A favorite word of mine, intention, escaped me.

I had no structure. I felt lost. What was I accomplishing? What was my *Why*? No one really needed me right now. I realized what kept me so busy in my previous employment—the pull of solving problems for a business, attending a meeting, the hum of sales follow-up. I was on a direct path to productivity in my old life. Here, in this new world of change, I needed to find my way.

CREATING STRUCTURE

I returned to the four sacred words that have always helped me bring my life onto the rails: *write out my day*. Here's what that process looks like:

- On Sunday, review your upcoming week.
- Check all your scheduled meetings in your calendar and the commitments you have made. Write them into a weekly paper calendar. What do you have to do the *day before* to ensure you are ready for that commitment? Fill it in.
- Fill in workouts and know how you will move your body each day.
- Is there anything you need to do for your family? Fill it in.
- Personal appointments?
- Major to-dos. This is the work that only you can do, like sales calls, email follow-up, social posts, writing, etc. Add

this information to a time block to ensure you get your work done.

You get the picture. Now, see the next bullets.

- Don't overwhelm yourself. Leave some white space for things to go wrong. A snow day. A sick kid. An accident at work. Too much traffic. A call from your parents or an old friend. Don't be so full that you have no room for life. Your discipline to get a few big things done each day will take you further in one week than you ever imagined.
- Go the extra mile and color code if you can: work, side hustle, kids/family, personal. This will give you a visual of where you are spending your time during the week.
- Each morning of the week, review this schedule. Can you stick to the plan? Did anything change? Do you need to move around something you didn't complete the day before? Make the change and commit to the plan.

A note on the time this activity should take: don't let this consume more than fifteen minutes. List making can cause paralysis and overthinking in some individuals. Don't let this be you! I start a timer on my phone or watch and complete this activity before it goes off. The last thing you want is to add an hour-long task to your to-do list to make another list!

This effort yields the most productive days for me. I don't let my phone, life's handiest tool and biggest distraction, get in my way. I have an awful habit of swiping right on my cell phone to look at the random assortment of news that Apple provides. These are mostly articles from *People* magazine, *InStyle*, and recommendations of the best travel pants to buy on Amazon. It's a black freaking hole. If I've made an appointment with myself to get the work done and can consistently commit to getting it done, I am golden. Show up for yourself consistently.

RECOVERING FROM SETBACKS

What do you do when you fall off the wagon? Get back on. It's like a snowball rolling for me. One day, if I don't do the things I say I'll do, I'll let the day run me. The next day, I have a pileup like a Houston, Texas, traffic jam where not only are you stuck on the highway surrounded by cars, but the Texas sun is melting you through the windows. I feel like that. So, I started compromising.

What do I not need to do? Those people don't really need to hear from me. I can wait one more week... it goes on and on. I'm a pro at it. Before I knew it, it was Friday, and I was nowhere near where I needed to be. It feels like make-or-break time. Get back on the wagon, stop the snowball, use Waze to find an alternate route, and do it quickly.

The best way I have found to make this happen is to go back to my routine of the calendar activity. It grounds me. My overwhelm melts, and I know one tiny step each day will eventually take me up the mountain.

Remember how intentional you were when you scheduled your week? It's easier to put things out of your mind and now worry about your to-do list all at once when you assign tasks to specific days and times. Train yourself to answer, "I'll do that on (insert day)." Pick up where you have left off, and don't jump ahead. Complete any important tasks you may have missed and move on!

CONSISTENCY CREATES WINNERS

Working in sales is the ultimate challenge in the consistency game. When I took a junior role in sponsorship sales in 2013, I had a big number staring at me on an Excel sheet. I had to sell a lot in less than a year. In fact, it was a goal number never by an individual in new business since the team's inception. Like any big goal, I did what they tell you to do and broke it down. I got my list of leads and figured out how many calls to make per day, how to follow up, and how to get a meeting. I knew my pitch to get in the door of a new client, and once I was there, I figured out what people responded to that would let me earn some of their advertising dollars.

I figured out a close percentage. How many proposals did I need to write to make that number? The number was one out of three if I had an even mix of large and small investment pitches. After an in person meeting with a potential client, one out of three advertising proposals would close. Diversity in spend was a necessary ingredient to this equation. I needed to add a few big deals to make the number, so I looked for the industries most likely to spend based on who had the largest advertising billboards at other ballparks or on the highway. Then, I went at them with my biggest pitch.

I clawed my way to the sales number. Strategy tells us we need a mixed bag. It should include those that spend big and partners whose initial buy-in is lower with an opportunity to grow. That way, year over year, you aren't searching for a whale of a deal that may or may not come. Plus, the more meetings you have, the more repetitions you get, the better you get at your job. All that consistent practice leads to achievement. I closed my last deal after the season started in April and made my number. It felt fantastic. The only way I got there was by consistently focusing on the task at hand: sales. I created a cycle of calls, emails, proposals, meetings, follow-up, closing a deal, completing a contract, and celebrating every day.

My ultimate challenge in consistency and patience was to show up and do the right thing every day. I saw several people around me get bored and distracted. They wanted something else to do and wasted their days talking to colleagues or spending too much time on a simple task to make the day melt away. Doing the same thing every day is boring. Find a way to stick with it (like knowing your *Why*), and you'll reap the reward in the end. If you know the goal and the reward, it's much easier to stay consistent in walking down the path.

My reward for consistently pursuing my sales goal was the commission, the personal satisfaction for reaching my goal, a promotion, and the company viewing me differently. I was a producer, and when you can add value, your voice gets bigger, and others give your thoughts and opinions more consideration, your confidence grows.

CONSISTENCY IN ACTION

Larra Overton is a host, reporter, and producer for the Indianapolis Colts. She joined the team in July 2019 after five years at Fox59 and CBS 4, most recently as sports reporter and anchor. She serves as the sideline reporter for the Colts radio broadcasts, hosts the weekly Colts 360 program, and produces multiple series for Colts Productions. In addition to her role with the Colts, she serves as a track and field analyst and sideline reporter for USATF, ESPN, and BTN.

After receiving her bachelor's degree in journalism and master's in sports communication from IU, she began her broadcasting career at Fox41 WDRB in Louisville, Kentucky. Larra moved to Indianapolis in 2010, working for the Pacers, Fox Sports, and the National Sports Journalism Center at IUPUI. After nine more years of consistent hard work and hustle, she got the offer from the Colts.

Larra's training for consistent pursuit of her goals started early in life while watching her mom coach the cheerleaders at the University of Louisville. She sat on the sidelines, observing the hard work of the athletes and her mom. Later, Larra had the good fortune of experiencing the push of a good coach when she became a track athlete. Sports was her example of how to consistently show up each day in pursuit of a goal.

Larra says, "When I knew I wanted to run in college, I chose Indiana, a BIG 10 school, where there were far better, faster, and more talented runners than me. I wanted to go to a place that would challenge me and bring out the best in me. That would push me outside my comfort zone. Track is hard. It's year-round. There were times I thought I would quit, and then I would have a breakthrough. Because I felt that challenge all through college, it instilled in me that insatiable hunger to keep going after more on a professional level."[1]

Larra's career is one of consistency. She has to show up every day to do the work and push herself to do just a little bit more. Stay the path. One foot in front of the other.

After graduation, she had to go out on her own and apply the skills she had learned to pursue the life she wanted. Consistency was key. It can be for you, too. Each day, do something to work toward your dream. Start today by making a commitment to do the work, one step at a time.

Dan Lier is a best-selling author and keynote speaker on consistency. He offers great advice on staying consistent. He says, "We set ourselves up for failure by setting a big goal and attacking it all at once. We condition our brains for success, and when we have success, the brain wants to do more. When we find ourselves failing, our mind shuts off and says, I quit."[2]

Dan adds, "The key to achieving your goals is to create consistency in many areas of your life. Create a habit, pattern of behavior, or hobby to get there. These success habits become micro goals to get to your ultimate goal. Bite-size chunks to create success habits."[3]

It's like writing this book. I didn't sit down and do it in one day. I wrote a chapter (or two!) each week. Week after week, consistently showing up to pursue the goal of completing and publishing a book. I did enlist a support team of editors to hold me accountable for my work, but it was up to me to sit at my computer, solo in my office, and put my fingers to the keys.

Marie Forleo, a successful entrepreneur, offers five steps to being consistent.

1. Keep your eye on the *why*! List the thing you want to do. Find *WHY* you love the thing you want to be consistent at, and then stick to it.
2. Pick your battle. Humans have a limited capacity when it comes to willpower. Progressively gain skills by focusing on only one at a time.
3. Schedule all your life around the thing you want to achieve and keep it at the top of your priority list. Steven Covey said, "Don't prioritize your schedule. Schedule your priorities."
4. Ignore your feelings. Ignore the voice in your head saying, *I don't feel like it.* Train yourself to override that voice in your head.
5. Catch the wagon. You are not a failure if you miss one day. Don't worry, and don't leave the practice if you miss one day or two.[4]

This is fantastic advice from the fabulous Marie, no surprise. She summed it up by saying, "Success doesn't come from what you do occasionally. It comes from what you do consistently."[5]

Commit to your goals and consistently pursue them. You should not shelve them for months and go back, dust them off, and try again. Consistency is key. Is it going to be hard? Yes. You stay even when it's hard. Think about your future self. What does that version of you feel six months from now? The goal is for your future self to feel grateful for the work you put in today. Grateful you are consistently pursuing your goal so, in six months, you won't believe how far you've progressed!

Stay consistent—keeping the promises you make to yourself develops confidence. You know you are a person of honor and integrity when you stay committed.

I'll let Dwayne "The Rock" Johnson sum it up for us. "Success isn't always about 'Greatness,' it's about consistency. Consistent, hard work gains success. Greatness will come."[6] The key to reaching any goal is consistency.

CONSISTENCY EXERCISE:

1. What is a goal you are currently working on? What do you want to achieve?
2. Why is it meaningful to you?
3. How can you show up for yourself consistently to ensure you get to the finish line?
4. How can you break down that goal into a smaller habit you can work on daily?
5. Write down your plan. Include a reasonable amount of time each week to work on your plan. Don't try to block off an entire day if this is unreasonable for your current schedule. One hour a week might be a good start for you. Remember your *why* and stick to the plan.
6. Get in the habit of scheduling your week to stay committed to your goal. Show up for yourself every day, and celebrate how far you've come.

TOP FOUR TAKEAWAYS:

1. **Achieving goals:** Consistency is the key to setting and achieving goals. By consistently working toward your goals, you develop a sense of discipline and form habits that support your progress. Consistent behavior

enables you to stay focused and ultimately reach your desired outcomes.

2. **Building trust and reliability:** Aside from the personal benefit of showing up for your goals consistently, it builds trust and reliability in your relationships. When you consistently follow through on commitments, people know they can count on you. Your reputation will soar when you remain consistent in your words and actions.

3. **Improving self-discipline:** Consistency in daily routines and habits helps develop self-discipline. When you practice self-discipline over and over, it becomes easier to resist distractions, overcome challenges, and make choices that align with your long-term goals.

4. **Enhancing overall well-being:** By consistently caring for your physical, mental, and emotional health, you create a foundation for improved energy and mood. You will have a better quality of life when you consistently show up for your dreams. One where you know you always have an opportunity to learn, change for the better, and grow, gaining more confidence in your abilities along the way.

CHAPTER 7

Increase Self-Control

——

For many people, self-control is the question of "Do I eat the brownie?" or—in my case—that stale donut in the box on the counter in the shared kitchen at work. It's looking delish right now. It's from yesterday, but I am in a real three pm slump with the sun hitting my eyes through the just right angle of my office window. If I have that donut, the sugar will get me moving.

I need some extra energy to get through the drive home, kid pick up, make dinner, bedtime, and check my email one more time. I should probably have a meaningful conversation with my husband and read the ten pages a day of a nonfiction book I committed to reading this month. It would be nice to find out what happens on *Dynasty* after that cliffhanger, too! What was I deciding on? Oh yeah, the damn donut!

The need for self-control occurs each day. The donut decision derailed about twenty minutes of work while I wondered if I should eat it, which then spiraled into my to-do list for the rest of the day. I can feel my heart racing as I type this, thinking about that anxiety bubbling up inside me from the temptation that led to a mind spiral.

It goes back to my goals and having self-control around them. Do I really need the donut? No. Perhaps some water and a little walk can get me the energy kick I need to get through the end of the day. Clearly, I need a break from sitting in front of my computer.

Having self-control is more than the donut. It's knowing your boundaries from the jump so you can resist the temptation and stay on track.

When I feel derailed, and distractions are popping up like the Minions on the newest version of Whac-A-Mole, I break it down into more bite-sized pieces. A really great trick I use is the timer on my Apple watch or phone. With the capabilities of this thing, I often feel like Dick Tracy.

Set your timer for twenty minutes and commit to staying committed to the task you need to finish.

My friend Paige told me about this trick she learned called *eat the frog*, where you do the most difficult thing first in your day. You get the tough stuff done before new distractions hit and feel that sense of accomplishment early. If you didn't eat your frogs in the morning and it's three in the afternoon, you are likely encountering the donut distraction, which makes it difficult to stay disciplined! Don't eat the donut. Eat the frog, and do it in twenty minutes.

I find I often turn the timer off and keep going, making progress on the task blowing past the finish line. I enter a state where I am far enough into the task when the timer goes off it has given me the momentum I need to get it done.

Self-control is a limited resource. Too much decision-making leads to decision fatigue, and the brain chooses a path of least resistance rather than the best choice.

I find decision fatigue is most overwhelming when my day is filled with too many meetings, so I'd like to address it here and provide some helpful guidance when you have a packed day. I'll use the meeting as an example of a preparedness framework. Preparedness equals confidence.

I have been a part of companies where they called on my leadership to attend meetings for more than four hours a day. This left little time to do my own work, and I found the more meetings I attended, the less effective the meetings became over time. This developed into bad habits and became a waste of time. Management lacked discipline to make decisions and had a tendency to push them off to the next meeting. Our low self-control leads us to fill the time allotted rather than use only the time we need. One-hour meetings were always exactly one hour when, if we had stuck to the task, we would have been able to wrap up sooner.

How do we run more effective meetings that do not deplete our self-control? *Preparation.*

Dedicating yourself to preparation is key to avoiding decision fatigue. Here is my best method for prep:

1. **Who?** Who is in the meeting, and why are they there? Make it clear, and don't waste people's time.
2. **Set the agenda and define the goal.** What is the proposed outcome? Why are we there, what will we discuss, what is standing in our way of progress, and finally, what decisions do we need to make?
3. **Share.** Share the agenda with all participants and require the pre-read, reviewing the agenda, and preparing notes for any areas you are responsible for. Everyone must come prepared, not just you.
4. **Pre-problem-solving.** Your brain is already working on problem-solving before you have entered the room. You will be able to make a decision with greater ease and not put your self-control tank on empty.

Preparing for meetings with a realistic assessment of objectives and expectations begins by applying these four steps. To be completely prepared, add intentionality and self-control to increase your confidence. To feel confident is to feel prepared.

They might call you demanding, but if you set the precedence that you will complete this four-step exercise for every meeting, I bet you'll find fewer meetings on your calendar because each meeting you hold will be more effective. Asking for this level of preparedness from your team and reminding them they are asking their coworkers to take time out of their day to attend is worth a discussion. Don't be the teammate who wastes people's time. That's a great way to go from an *all-star* to *benchwarmer*.

You can apply these preparation steps to many areas of your life, not just meetings. It's the act of being prepared that increases your self-control.

SELF-CONTROL STRATEGIES

Self-control has us stop doing an activity we already do, perhaps in the middle of it. It is the ability to control yourself in difficult or tempting situations. Self-discipline, as discussed in Chapter 3, gets us to begin a new task or project and stick with it. They go hand-in-hand. Once you apply self-control, self-discipline can redirect a person's actions.

Effective self-control strategies include:

- focusing on one goal at a time (too much at one time will leave you chasing a purple squirrel and never making real progress.)
- planning for situations that might break your resolve, and
- avoiding temptation wherever possible.

Self-control requires self-awareness and the capacity to delay gratification, making deliberate choices that align with your goals.

What are some areas of your life where self-control could be implemented to improve your performance?

To give you some ideas on where to start, I'll share the most recent area where I have used greater control to help me reach my goals.

I need good sleep, so I don't use Instagram after eight in the evening. Let's face it. Nothing great ever came from scrolling Instagram at that time. I have bought backpacks I don't use, low-quality sweaters from influencers, and looked at posts when I was tired, which made me lose motivation. It's easy to get into a comparison trap after a long day, and who wants to sleep on those bad feelings? Blue light and brain stimulation at this hour worked me up, woke me up, and distracted me from my main goal, getting good sleep.

A big step here was to identify what was stealing my willpower around self-control. In this case, poor sleep habits. The culprit here? Instagram. Creating this boundary helped me to stop thinking about whether I should or shouldn't open it up, and battle lost time, usually over a half hour, I could not get back. No more decisions were necessary. I just don't open Instagram after eight in the evening. Instead, I talk with my husband, spend time reading or playing games with my boys, watch a TV show with my family, play a once-a-week intramural kickball game, call a friend, or read a book. Anything to decompress from the day and connect with the people around me offline.

The people with the best self-control resist temptation so they can put self-discipline into practice. What can you identify that's stealing your self-control?

Efficiency queen Sloane Logue, who works professionally as a Talent Agent at WME, loves discipline and knows how to get things done quickly. She does not let distractions get in her way. One of her favorite tips is to schedule her emails. She says, "I work a lot on Sunday afternoons to get caught up, but I don't want anyone to answer me on Sundays, so I schedule them to go out at the right time Monday morning, depending on their time zone."[1]

Sloane offers a second email tip, "Inbox pause. For an hour or for however long I want to schedule it, I can't get an email so I can work on those projects or the PowerPoint I need to do or read a contract... It's easy to just look at your inbox and respond. Then it is three hours later, and you've yet to finish your work."[2] She also suggests, like Paige, to use your first hour of the morning to do your hard stuff. You get it done, it's over, and you have got the hard stuff out of the way when you have more energy.

We've got to reduce the number of decisions we make each day to continue performing at our highest and best. Avoiding distractions to the best of our ability (hello airplane mode!) and making fewer decisions about the things that are not as important are the keys to avoiding the decision fatigue that weakens our self-control.

Imagine choosing your outfit at the start of your day. You shift foot to foot, your eyes surveying the entirety of your closet. You acknowledge it, saying to yourself, "I am wasting so much time right now staring at these clothes." You try on three outfits, you don't like any of them, and drop the clothes on your floor. That's more to rehang later, sucking up more of your time. You realize this happens every day, and in this moment, you might come up with a few strategies to avoid this situation next time like:

1. Placing all your work clothes in one area of the closet. Organize them by tops and bottoms so that comfy sweatshirt and yoga pants can't pull you into the thoughts of how badly you wish you could wear them to the office!
2. After laundry, you rehang your clothes as outfits. Two birds, one stone.
3. You plan to spend one hour organizing over the weekend. Set a timer. Organizing will help you to plan ahead for situations that may break your resolve, steal your time, and cause you to make too many decisions.

… This is probably why Mark Zuckerberg wears the same thing every day.

In Melanie Curtin's article for *Inc.* Magazine, she tells us the average human is only productive for about three to four hours of a work day.[3] For some people it's only two to three! This is an astounding stat given our culture's dedication to an eight-hour workday.

Distractions tempt us all, most commonly digital temptations. Right now, I've had a thought pop into my head. I am typing on my computer, which has an internet connection, and the internet contains a black hole of searchable information, shopping at our fingertips, and answers to our greatest curiosities.

What tempts you during the day by distraction? How can you limit this temptation? Is there a rule you can set around this temptation that will keep you on track?

Tip: Don't think too hard. The majority of your distractions come from a minority of sources. In my case, I'd say text messages. I checked my phone usage, and texting was the highest use category! Next comes social media scrolling. Then, emails from companies who want me to buy their products. Here are some rules you can use to manage task-switching temptation and up your level of self-control:

- Batch answer texts instead of one on one. Schedule time in your calendar to tackle text messages instead of dropping what you are doing to respond instantly.
- Create rules around social media. I ask myself, why am I opening this app? If it's not an appropriate time to look something up, post, or engage, then it's a no. Having the discipline to eliminate mindless scrolling is a game-changer for my time and mental health.
- Batch delete emails from companies who are trying to sell me something. I open my email in my browser window. Click on the promotions tab. Scroll to see if you need to save anything in that tab that is possibly categorized incorrectly (like a hotel reservation), and then I hit the checkbox and delete them all. I am not kidding. This has saved more than thirty minutes in my day because I previously developed a habit of checking these messages like they were work emails! Just like that, a half-hour more per day to go after my biggest goals.

It feels like distractions are insurmountable. My phone is going off constantly. My connected watch, too. All these tools help me to lead a productive life but also serve as the ultimate distraction. Developing habits of self-control around technology is key to using this tech to help, not hinder, your life. Self-control breeds confidence. When you are sure you can control your actions and stick to your plans, confidence soars.

In Megan Marple's article for CNN, she discussed how decision fatigue drains you of your energy to make thoughtful choices. From the moment you wake up, decisions face you. Deciding what to wear and what's for breakfast. Maybe you have children who are asking you questions, and you are picking out their outfits and feeding them, too. Your email is going off, texts are entering, and you decide which route to take to work.[4]

"Your brain is making upward of 35,000 decisions each day," according to Eva Krockow, lecturer at the University of Leicester in the United Kingdom. "By the evening, you're exhausted, but you can't quite put your finger on why."[5] Making too many decisions can impair your judgment and encourage you to make a decision too quickly, depending on your self-control.

Anders Ericsson, a Swedish psychologist and researcher who is known for his work on the science of expertise and the concept of deliberate practice, has written extensively on the subject of how individuals can achieve high levels of performance in their chosen fields through focused, goal-oriented practice.[6]

Using Ericsson's ideas, rather than expecting to be prolifically focused, fence off four hours a day of uninterrupted work time each day. Block off this time for the work *only you can do* and save the rest of the day to answer emails, have external meetings, research, etc.

Consider the battery of self-control. You only have so much battery on any given day. My sleep, exercise, outside environment, and daily meetings, including who I get to or have to talk to, all play into how big of a battery I get to use up each day. Do your best to create an environment for yourself where you can succeed.

DECISION FATIGUE CURES:
1. Simplify your environment. Create a routine or utilize a system or software to reduce the number of temptations in your day.
   - Plan a simplified wardrobe, create a morning routine (do the same things each morning to prepare yourself for the day), and commit to a weekly workout schedule on Sunday (know what you are committing to for exercise each day, so you don't have to decide when you are tired!)
   - Several apps can help you reach your goals and make decisions for you. For example, an app called Run Keeper creates a marathon training plan (or any distance race you'd like to run) that will tell you exactly how many miles, how fast, and how often you need to run to reach your race goal.
   - Utilize CRM software. With your input, this software will create a daily follow-up plan for you to reach your sales goals.
2. Prioritize: do the most important things first when your energy level is high.

3. Take a break between tasks. Commit to working on one project for an hour and know when that hour is up. You will take a break and do a short activity to recharge you for your next segment of work, like walking the dogs, making a snack, answering texts, calling a friend, working out, meditating, etc.
4. Be aware of how you feel. Are you stressed or overwhelmed? Know yourself and what you need to calm down. A frazzled mind is no help to those around you or your committed goal-getting self.

Consider the amount of time you really need. Are you doing too much? Are you a manager who can assign work or recruit help? Can some of your work create a volunteer or intern opportunity in your office? Have you ever caught yourself sealing envelopes? Guilty! I send annual Christmas cards with handwritten notes both from home and the office. I found myself writing, stuffing, addressing, and posting the office notes the same way I'd done at home. It took several hours to do everything beyond the writing. I could have assigned that task to a team member I managed and saved time during my day for only the work I, as the boss, could do.

Elisa Padilla, Chief Marketing Officer at New York Red Bulls, says, "I went to work every day like I was the intern, even when I was Chief Marketing Officer, I rolled up my sleeves... When you are a leader, and you are leading a team, you have to lead by example. Critical for me as I was going up the ladder was I never wanted to ask someone to do something I didn't know how to do or I didn't understand the process because if I didn't know or if they get pushback, how am I going to be able to lead that person in the process?"[7]

You might feel a slight resistance from within when assigning a task to a teammate, but remember, as Elisa says, you are the leader. You have been in those shoes. You did the work and can use your experience to guide them through the process and give them the opportunity to learn and grow through a task you used to complete. Do it all once, then delegate.

Don't take on too much. Evaluate where you spend your time and discover what you can take off your plate.

SELF-CONTROL ASSESSMENT:

1. Where are some areas of your life where self-control could be implemented to improve your performance?
2. What can you identify that's stealing your self-control? Make a list. It might be long. Take time to review the list and consider where you can create a plan for efficiency. What can you stop doing? What can you assign? What can you outsource? What can you do to plan ahead so you are not wasting your time on this item daily?
3. What tempts you during the day by distraction? How can you limit this temptation? Is there a rule you can set around this temptation that will keep you on track?
4. Are you feeling stressed or overwhelmed? Are you doing too much? Are you a manager who can assign work or recruit help? Can some of your work create a volunteer or intern opportunity in your office?

TOP FOUR TAKEAWAYS:

1. **Overcoming self-doubt:** Self-control allows us to resist negative self-talk and self-sabotaging behaviors (the donut!) that can hinder our confidence. We can complete

more empowering thoughts and actions to build belief in ourselves and our abilities.

2. **Consistency in pursuing goals:** Self-confidence often comes from achieving goals. Self-control is crucial for maintaining consistent effort toward these goals. It helps us stay disciplined, manage distractions, and follow through with necessary actions, ultimately leading to improved confidence through the accomplishment of meeting our goals or learning valuable lessons along the way of pursuing our goals.

3. **Managing emotions:** Self-control enables us to regulate our emotions in challenging situations. When faced with setbacks or criticism, it's easy to feel discouraged and lose confidence. However, by exercising self-control, we can control impulsive reactions, maintain composure, and respond more positively. This emotional resilience fosters confidence as we learn to adapt and handle difficult circumstances.

4. **Developing self-discipline:** Confidence often stems from a sense of personal competence and mastery. By practicing self-control, we develop self-discipline, which allows us to build competence and expertise in our lives. Increased proficiency bolsters our confidence, as we have evidence of our own capabilities and accomplishments, leading to stronger belief in ourselves.

CHAPTER 8

Abandon Perfection

In second grade, I rode home in our old baby blue Oldsmobile and admired the neon sunset out the window. It was breathtaking for a summertime sky, orange, yellow, red, and the slightest bit of purple as it turned from day to night. Inspired, I thought, *When I get home, I will draw this sunset!*

We parked in the garage, and I went right to my room and unboxed my new neon crayons. What a treat! I had all the brand-new colors I needed to make the most perfect sunset picture. As I pulled out my piece of paper, I imagined all the praise I would receive when I showed my family. Maybe I'd then win some sort of coloring contest that awarded a free trip to Hawaii, where I could spend each evening creating a similar photo but of the exotic sky from the beaches of a faraway island.

I got to work. I looked out the window for inspiration, with the sunset slowly fading away. The colors I had were perfect.

Twenty minutes later, I studied my masterpiece. It looked like a neon-striped shirt. The beautiful image I had in my mind would have to stay there—in my mind—because I was incapable of translating it to paper. My dreams were dead, and my new crayons were wasted on this terrible drawing!

Yet, here I am thirty years later, writing about a time I tried out some new art techniques and failed miserably according to my type A perfectionist standards. Since then, I have drawn many more crappy pictures for fun and enjoyed doing art with my kids, made up sketches of my thoughts for a graphic designer, or tried my own hand in Canva to promote my clients and my businesses.

I have seen perfection stand in the way of progress more times than I can count; this could have been one of them. Yet this example of an eight-year-old attempting to draw a sunset has stuck with me. Would perfection be the end of drawing for good? No, and it shouldn't be for you either. A rough draft is all you need.

When I started my podcast, *Leadership is Female*, I had no idea what I was doing. I didn't have podcast equipment or a soundproof room. I had a computer and a white wobbly desk from Wayfair. I signed up for a course to teach me about online marketing, and one of the segments, just a single week, was about podcasting. During this week of curriculum, I remember thinking, "I can't start a podcast." As much as I was resisting the opportunity because of the fear of not being perfect, I knew deep down that the podcast would be my takeaway from the class.

No equipment. Little time. No money to invest in an editor. Terrible Chicago accent. You name it. I had an excuse.

However, the idea kept biting at the back of my brain. Do it, Emily! Start a podcast.

I discovered, or maybe remembered when I thought back to that sunset drawing, I had permission to "make it messy" and "do C+ work." I'm an *A* student and a neat freak, but the voice in my head told me to go for it and pushed me to adopt a non-perfect mentality.

I vividly remember sitting on the carpet of my closet floor and staring at the one-minute teaser reel that would introduce the podcast I'd recorded at least fifteen different times. It was short, snappy, and succinct. I wondered if I should try recording another version. Would it be better? The clock had ticked past two hours that I'd been sitting on that floor, just to ready the short introduction. I'd never make progress on my goal if perfection had me in its handcuffs.

I spoke to myself aloud, "Emily, are you going to do this or what? Give yourself twenty seconds of courage and hit the publish button." I moved my mouse over "publish," took a deep breath, and depressed the trackpad. The podcast was live.

I made it messy. I gave myself permission not to be perfect.

I figured out how to record on my MacBook and discovered a way to publish podcasts to all the major networks for free. My first interview featured a fantastic guest who gave a phenomenal interview, but my voice and my style make me cringe when I listen back today. However, I wouldn't change it. Ninety percent of podcasters do not record more than ten episodes. Today, tens of thousands of people have heard the interviews on *Leadership is Female* and is ranked in the top 200 business podcasts worldwide, because I gave myself permission not to be perfect. I applied twenty seconds of courage. The women who share their stories and voices have a platform, which means so much to me and my listeners.

Consider if the idea of perfection might be standing in the way of achieving your goals.

- What could you accomplish if you gave yourself permission to abandon perfection?
- What could you start?
- What could you finish?
- What goals could you chip away at daily?

JUST GO FOR IT

Melanie Newman is an American radio and television play-by-play broadcaster for the Baltimore Orioles of Major League Baseball and the national Friday Night Baseball broadcasts on Apple TV+. She is the first woman to be a play-by-play announcer for the Orioles and one of only four female play-by-play broadcasters active in MLB in 2023.

I met Melanie Newman through a friend of a friend, and I interviewed her in 2021 from my office at the ballpark in Reno. She was in her apartment in Somewhere, USA, preparing to leave for spring training. She was full of energy, and others have always described her as an energetic and versatile broadcaster. She has a big smile, big hair, big lashes, and a big brain. She's one of the smartest people in the room, and her ability to study, recall, and entertain is unmatched.

She made her way into baseball, an industry dominated by men, one minor league season at a time. She rode the bus with the players on the Double-A Mobile Bay Bears and showed she'd put in the time and the effort with the right mentality. If Melanie had expected perfection from herself from the start, she never would have started at all. She gave herself the time and space to succeed, putting herself in a position to grow over time. She worked her way up through the minor leagues just like a ballplayer. Her path led to success, all the while believing she belonged.

For Melanie to overcome her desire for perfection, the first thing she did was pursue a career that excited her—a career in broadcasting, her first love. Her dream burned so brightly inside of her that she was willing to do anything to pursue it.

Melanie said, "You have to stick to your guns and know this is where you are meant to be regardless of what people on the outside say to you."[1]

She shared, "I didn't grow up knowing I wanted to be a broadcaster, and I struggled with that identity for a long time because I had heard other broadcasters say they had known since they were six. It made me feel like I didn't deserve to be here for a while. It makes you realize that human life has so many different forms of how you find your way. You can't play the comparison game, especially when it comes to hitting big career marks."[2]

Did she know she'd be a trailblazer? Did she know she'd hold so many first titles as a woman like:

- First woman to be a play-by-play announcer for the Orioles
- First all-female broadcast team to host an MLB game for YouTube
- First-time all-female broadcast team to call a nationally televised Major League Baseball game

She didn't let perfection stand in her way. Perfection would mean she'd never hold a microphone because how could she ever be perfect on her first or second try? Melanie's mentality to keep going, to continue to build her confidence through diligent practice, and not to let perfection stand in her way brought her dreams to life.

Melanie offered a final piece of advice during our interview, "Stick to your guns and believe you belong."[3] This sentiment describes a mentality that no matter what, no matter how imperfectly you perform at the beginning, you won't quit. Keep practicing, keep trying, make it messy, put yourself out there, and the opportunities will come.

THE RESEARCH SHOWS: PERFECTION WILL RUIN YOU

Charly Haversat gave a TEDx Talk about how perfectionism holds us back. Her hook, "Can we fight the crippling fear of failure and the unwillingness to compromise that it creates?" She hits on a conundrum that's troubled great thinkers, at least back to the Enlightenment. The Nirvana Fallacy, dating back to the 1700s, is the informal fallacy of comparing actual things with unrealistic, idealized alternatives or the tendency to assume there is a perfect solution to a particular problem. Charly says, "Voltaire argued the 'perfect is the enemy of the good,' but we came to say, 'If I can't do it perfectly, I won't do it all.'"[4]

Today, we think perfect is not only possible but probable, and in this mindset, we have lost our ability to negotiate incremental gains. Many have stopped trying at all. The Nirvana Fallacy has created cultures where we are afraid to fail.

In Tracy Bower's article for *Forbes*, she cites an important stat, "If you try to be perfect, you're in good company. A study of over 41,000 people published in the *Psychological Bulletin* found perfectionism has increased over time, partly because of the comparisons people make with each other on social media, and partly because of the competitive environments that colleges and employers are increasingly creating."[5]

Setting impossibly high standards for yourself is bad for your health and can lead to burnout, depression, and anxiety, but society continues to plant the idea in our minds that perfection is attainable for some. The truth is perfectionism will hold you back. It's a trap! Trying to be perfect is demotivating. You'll feel like you will never be good enough and, in turn, will miss out on the rewards of accomplishment. Additionally, perfectionism will distance you from others when they see your impossibly high standards and think they will never measure up. Your effectiveness reduces when you try to be perfect. Progress stifles, and you won't benefit from incremental gains if you can't submit your work to receive feedback.

Thankfully, Tracy's article goes on to give advice on how to be less of a perfectionist.

- *Change your mind.* The old adage is true, "Change your thinking, change your life." Recognize that you're limiting yourself and seek to think differently—taking the pressure off yourself to be all things to all people all the time. Know you can't possibly do it all and reassure yourself that whatever you do well is a contribution to the community and to your colleagues. When you realize you can't do everything and can't do it perfectly, you actually liberate yourself to focus. You can choose what you'll prioritize and where you'll invest your energy rather than spreading yourself so thin that you fail to feel good about anything.

- *Find a Friend.* Change is always easier when you go through it with a buddy. Find a trusted colleague with whom you can compare notes and who can give you feedback and validate your efforts, as well as challenge you when you're getting stuck. Check-in regularly and share how things are going. The process of reflecting with a friend and feeling known and understood can help you make progress.

- *Be Selective.* Another way to manage perfection is by assessing what's most important for your performance and growth. There may be tasks that are less important or less consequential—and you can put less into those—while other tasks demand a higher level of effort. Consider the way pilots fly: They use autopilot for the more mundane aspects of a flight, but they are hands-on for maneuvers that are more complex, such as takeoff and landing. You'll want to do quality work in everything, but you can be intentional about which elements of your work get the highest levels of exertion.

- *Set Deadlines.* It is true that "Work expands to fit available time," so set deadlines for your projects. Remember those meetings that always filled the full hour? Give yourself a timeframe for your work, and when you hit the limit, call the outcome good enough. Strive to do your best and be ready to say something is good enough when it's time to complete the task.
- *Adopt a Mantra.* It can be helpful to adopt a saying which will help you stay focused on your goal. Pick something that works for you and use it to reinforce the new behavior you want to adopt. For example, tell yourself, "Done is better than perfect." Or "Don't confuse excellence with perfection." Keep these in mind as you seek to change your beliefs and your behaviors.[6]

Give yourself permission to pursue *good enough*, not perfection. Can we shift the focus to consider how far we've come rather than try to do it perfectly on the first try?

I can understand the need, the want, to be perfect. Today, we feel so publicly judged. So much of what we do is available to be reviewed and critiqued online, and we want to do our best. But going for a perfect ten on your first attempt is nearly impossible and sets a standard for yourself that does not even allow you to try.

Make it messy. Allow yourself to get going and try before you set higher expectations for your work. Remember when you were a child and how you'd try just about anything. Your teacher would set out an art project for the entire class.

Thirty kids would work on making an owl out of a paper bag, and every final product was unique and different. We allowed ourselves to try early in life, so give yourself that same opportunity today.

Remember, no one is perfect, regardless of what stage of life they're in. Our imperfections are what make us beautifully human, and confidence stems from embracing and celebrating our unique selves. So, let go of perfection, allow your authentic self to shine, and watch your confidence soar.

CONSIDER WHAT IMPERFECTION MEANS TO YOU AND TAKE YOUR FIRST STEP:

1. What would you try if no one were watching? What have you always wanted to try? Would it be possible to try in the same way you tried an imperfect cartwheel at five years old? When you didn't care if anyone was watching or what they thought, you just thought it would be fun.
2. Give yourself twenty seconds of courage. What if you only had to be brave for a total of twenty seconds? What would you try?
3. Name a goal to complete in the next three months. Set it on your calendar for ninety days from now. Work backward with what you'll need to do each week to get there. Today, take your first step.

Stop pursuing perfection and start taking the next imperfect step toward reaching your goals.

TOP FOUR TAKEAWAYS:

1. **Embracing imperfection helps to create self-acceptance:** Perfection is an unattainable goal. When we abandon the pursuit of perfection, we allow ourselves to embrace our flaws, uniqueness, and imperfections. It is through this self-acceptance that true confidence flourishes. Confidence is not about being flawless; it's about being authentic and comfortable in our own skin.

2. **Perfection is paralyzing:** Striving for perfection often leads to unproductive procrastination, anxiety, and self-doubt. It's like trying to climb an insurmountable mountain where we will never reach the summit. We free ourselves from this paralyzing mindset when we abandon the need to be perfect. We become more willing to take risks, make mistakes, and learn from them. Our confidence grows as we understand failure and imperfection are essential stepping stones on the path to success.

3. **Connection thrives in imperfection:** Perfect is boring. When we let go of the unrealistic expectation always to be flawless, we open ourselves up to deeper and more authentic connections with others. Vulnerability is at the heart of meaningful relationships. Through our imperfections, we allow others to relate to us on a genuine level. By embracing imperfection, we create an environment that invites others to do the same, fostering a sense of belonging and boosting our confidence in the process.

4. **Flexibility and growth require imperfection:** Life is full of unexpected twists and turns. Adapting to changes and continuously growing as individuals requires a willingness to let go of the pursuit of perfection. We open

ourselves up to new possibilities and opportunities we may have missed otherwise. By embracing imperfection, we become more flexible, resilient, and adaptable, key ingredients for a confident and successful life.

CHAPTER 9

Deal With Failure

———

On my first day of work, I was nervous. Thirteen new college grads from around the country and I began our ticket sales internship in Chicago in June. We were working for the Chicago Bulls!

For a girl from the way north suburbs, this thrilled me. My brothers and I watched the Bulls achieve two three-peats (a third consecutive championship) on our living room TV. We banged on pots and pans with wooden spoons, cheering them on to victory. The next morning, we'd beg my mom to stop at the pop-up T-shirt stand on the gas station corner to buy our championship T-shirts featuring the team's stars, including the legend Michael Jordan.

I had a twin bed in the corner of a Wrigleyville apartment just four blocks from the Addison El Stop, which I shared with my high school friend, who was gracious enough to let me room with her. I had a new green button-up shirt from Express, a black suit coat, and flared suit pants. Complete with my pumps from Payless, I was ready to go for my first day. I wore the whole outfit for my four-block walk to where I boarded the train.

The El was at least 95 degrees, and following my half-mile walk, I was sweating bullets to begin my forty-five-minute commute to the West Loop. I rode uncomfortably, standing on my heels, feeling the sweat pooling in their pointy toes. I changed to a bus at Madison Street and felt the sweet relief of air conditioning. I hoped I'd cool off and dry my sweat-stained shirt before I greeted my new colleagues.

The bus pulled up and announced, "United Center!" I grabbed my purse and black folder and stepped off the bus. I was looking at a massive fence with the stadium in the middle. Where do I go in? I chose to walk west to what looked like ticket windows, and because of the building's mass, the destination was about half a block away. I arrived at the ticket windows. No one was there! I could see some doors on the other side of the fence that looked promising.

I looked down at my heels, and the plastic tips on these shoes were starting to look like a used eraser. I began to walk in the same direction I came from. Another half block down and then half block up to the doors. I pulled on the handle, and it opened! I stepped inside, took off my jacket, revealing my sweaty green shirt, and exclaimed, "Thank God!"

I looked over to see the entire class sitting on chairs. I was the last to arrive and a total mess. I bashfully mumbled, "I'm Emily," and my new boss said, "Great, now that you have arrived, let's take our badge photos." My first city commute made for a rocky start to my "dream job."

When I'd pass the Michael Jordan statue each morning as I entered the United Center, I felt I was living a dream. My job included two tickets to every game. The other interns and I would sit in an unsold suite above the 300 level, practically hanging from the rafters. The players looked like ants on the court, but I was part of the *action*... something I had wanted since I was a kid... Big city life and constant excitement! My dream was to work in sports, and I had finally got my chance.

I had one problem. I took a position where my primary goal each day was to make eighty phone calls to people I didn't know and try to sell them season tickets. This was my nightmare!

Talk to people I didn't know?

Sell them something!

Ask for money?

They told me "No" more times than I could count. People have laughed at me and often hung up on me.

What was I thinking when I accepted this job?

After nine months, the internship was coming to a close. Daily, I showed up, made my calls, and sold my heart out. I battled demons, including the fear of making calls, competition with classmates, nights out on the town and showing up on time the next morning, the boredom of repetitive calls, and worrying about my future. Was this what working in sports was?

I gave it my all anyway. When I knew I wouldn't make my weekly sales goal, I at least vowed to be the hardest worker in the group and make the most calls that week to earn a hefty bonus of one hundred dollars.

In mid-February, on a Friday night, we got the email. They selected two people from our class of fourteen to join the full-time staff. None of the names on the list were mine.

I lost, and I cried. I failed. When I thought about it, I wasn't even sure if my dream was to keep working in sports or just win the position at the end of the internship. I decided that less than one year into my new career as an intern-to-be-sports executive, I would change careers and look for work at a large nonprofit.

When I announced my new job to my boss, he told me it was a terrible decision. "Once you leave, you'll never get back in," were his parting words.

However, he didn't know somewhere in those nine months of sitting in a cubicle not much wider than my shoulders, I had grown confident in myself and the belief I could do anything I set my mind to do. I had grown more in those nine months than I ever thought possible. Each day, I pushed out of my comfort zone to improve on a new skill.

My next role was working for the Muscular Dystrophy Association in Chicago. A cause where I believed I could make a difference.

I was doing work outside the office, building partnerships with firefighters to Fill-the-Boot, making cold calls to city professionals to raise money for our lunchtime events, discovering how to partner with the sports teams in town through jersey auctions and raffle ticket sales, and meeting with law partners to start the next golf tournament. It was a good spot for me to grow into my next chapter.

Losing sucks. But after a loss, there is an opportunity. One to pick yourself up and find the next right fit. Let loss show itself as a four-way intersection. One where you have a chance to pick a new direction. Don't let it tell you no. Let it help set the course for who you were meant to be.

OPPORTUNITIES GROW FROM LOSSES

The darkness of failure feels crushing.

Katie Holloway Bridge is a four-time Paralympic athlete in Sitting Volleyball for Team USA. Katie told me in an interview on the *Leadership is Female* podcast, "Being a part of Team USA is a unique experience that only a small group of people get to be a part of. The first time I went to Beijing, it was amazing. I was awestruck. I fell in love. We didn't perform well, but I was hooked. For the second games, I was training full time, and we went to London. I expected to get to the gold medal match and win... and we lost. And that was very, very hard to come back from and very depressing."[1]

Olympic athletes often have their entire identity tied to their performance and their personal success in their sport. It's what they work toward every day, and losing or failing can be an incredibly difficult circumstance to get over.

After 2016 and the loss in London, Katie did the work to uncouple her identity from her performance as an athlete. She said, "I am a whole person, I am a separate person, I have purpose outside of sport. We don't teach that to athletes because the identity of a person is defined through the athlete. The pressure leads to a lack of enjoyment of the journey. It's hard to see what's in front of you and have any perspective other than your next competition."[2] When that's over, or an athlete fails to reach the pinnacle, it's incredibly difficult to overcome.

Katie created a life outside of her sport as a full-time employee, wife, and now mother. This gave her purpose and other people to serve beside her teammates. Being a Paralympian was no longer her whole life.

You can apply Katie's athlete example to any of our failures. Perspective is the key. It's wonderful to give it your all in your career. However, you have to consider your whole life, too.

Losing the full-time job with the Bulls was a huge failure, and I took it hard, but when I put it in perspective, I still had my family, my friends, my health, and a resume that would help me find the next opportunity.

If we keep going forward, one step at a time, our failures can become our launching pads.

THE SCIENCE OF FAILURE

In his TEDx Talk, Astro Teller turned to science for a dose of larger perspective. He's the head of X (formerly Google X) and gave a talk on the TED stage called "The Unexpected Benefit of Celebrating Failure." He talked about the "moonshot factory," where his team seeks to solve the world's biggest problems through experimental projects like balloon-powered internet and wind turbines that sail through the air.[3]

Astro's advice? Run at all the hardest parts of the project first. He told his audience to think, "How am I going to kill this project today? A balance between unchecked optimism to fuel our visions but then harness enthusiastic skepticism to breathe reality into your projects."[4]

Astro's team has learned a tremendous amount from attempting to complete projects that solve big problems like vertical farming and a lighter-than-air cargo ship. They killed both projects. But that didn't stop the team. They allowed themselves to fail, used what they learned, and endeavored on other projects.[5]

Astro says, "A major flaw or failure can actually put you on a more productive path. Failure can shift your perspective." and "Being audacious and working on big, risky things makes people inherently uncomfortable. You cannot yell at people and force them to fail fast. They worry about what will happen to me if I fail? Will people laugh at me? Will I be fired?"[6]

Astro goes on, "The only way to get people to work on big risky things, audacious ideas, and have them run at all the hardest parts of the problem first is if you make that the path of least resistance for them. We work hard at X to make it safe to fail. Teams kill their ideas as soon as the evidence is on the table because they get rewards for it. They get applause from their peers and hugs and high-fives from their manager. They get a promotion for it. They get bonuses for it." He went on to say, "Enthusiastic skepticism is not the enemy of boundless optimism. It's optimism's perfect partner. It unlocks the potential in every idea."[7]

Imagine applying this to your life. Consider how failure can shift your perspective. Often, we have to leave our current situations to gain perspective. Was my losing a full-time job after an internship really the end of the world? Nope. I was only twenty-two. Life was just beginning. Was Katie losing in the London Games at the end of her time as a Paralympian? Nope. In fact, she went on to compete in two more, won a gold medal, and most importantly, the loss in London triggered her to find her identity apart from being an athlete.

Can you imagine if we lived in a world that celebrated failure? What would you try?

Failure gives us a chance. A chance to try something new. It opens doors, changes your course, and puts you right where you were meant to be. Use failure to propel yourself forward down your next right path.

Failure can provide valuable lessons and insights that success often lacks. By experiencing failure, you can identify what went wrong, analyze your mistakes, and learn how to improve. It serves as a teacher that helps build resilience, adaptability, and problem-solving skills. Emphasize the importance of embracing failure as a stepping stone toward personal growth and fulfilling your potential.

Failure can be liberating as it helps you confront and conquer your fears. It encourages you to step outside your comfort zone and take risks, leading to personal development and self-discovery. By sharing personal stories of overcoming fear, you can inspire confidence in others to face their own challenges head-on and seize opportunities, regardless of the potential for failure. When it feels tough to move forward, consider how you may give others permission to get up and try again because they saw your example.

Moving forward will test your resilience and ability to bounce back from setbacks. Sharing stories of personal failure can help emphasize that setbacks are temporary and you achieve success through perseverance and determination. Change your perspective to view failures as stepping stones on the path to success rather than roadblocks that hinder progress. Resilience and perseverance lead to personal achievements and increased self-confidence.

Failure will challenge you to reassess your goals. As goal-getting people, we don't want to fail, but it allows for self-reflection and the opportunity to pursue more meaningful and fulfilling paths. Maybe your original target no longer serves you? Not reaching your goal can, conversely, be a catalyst for personal growth, enabling you to discover new passions and redefine your own version of success.

Embrace failure as a chance to evaluate your values, passions, and priorities.

This temporary loss can ultimately lead to a more confident and fulfilling life.

HOW TO OVERCOME FAILURE
Start by considering the following:

- What is one major failure in your career? Give yourself permission to feel the emotions. Failure hurts! Reflect on those feelings and emotions. Name it. It's critical to your success.
- Practice self-compassion. Extend the same compassion to yourself that you would give to others. Imagine your best friend telling you about his or her failure. How would you respond to that friend?
- Consider what you learned. Reflecting on the experience and identifying what you have learned can help you to foster resilience in the future.
- Adopt a growth mindset. How did you use those learnings to find your next opportunity? Believe you can grow and develop over time by making it through hard situations. Failure does not mean you are not good enough. It might mean you just haven't figured it out yet and need to give yourself the grace to learn, or the opportunity wasn't right for you at that time.
- Revisit your goals and make a plan for the future. It's okay to let go of a goal that no longer serves you. It's important that you choose a goal that aligns with your current values and plan.

TOP FOUR TAKEAWAYS:

1. **Adopt a growth mindset:** Recognize that failures are not indicative of your worth or abilities. See failure as an opportunity for growth and improvement rather than a reflection of personal shortcomings.

2. **Seek support and feedback:** Reach out for support from mentors, peers, or friends during challenging times. Seeking feedback and different perspectives can provide valuable insights and encourage personal and professional development.

3. **Practice self-compassion:** Self-compassion is paramount. Self-doubt and negative self-talk accompany failure. Treat yourself with kindness and understand failure is a natural part of the learning process.

4. **Set realistic goals and celebrate progress:** Set realistic goals that align with their values and passions. Break your goals into smaller milestones and celebrate each accomplishment, even if you may not achieve your desired outcome immediately. This helps build confidence and motivation to persevere through failures and setbacks.

CHAPTER 10

Check Your Self-Talk

My brain isn't always so nice. It will tell me things like, "This is too hard," "Other people can do it better," "You're an amateur," "You'll never get there," and other self-deprecating phrases. You know what they call it: self-doubt, imposter syndrome, negative self-talk, and being too hard on yourself. I'm convinced we all do it and I wonder why our brains wiring is this way. Why don't our brains' automatically give pump-up speeches championing us to blissfully surmount our biggest hurdles with exclamations like, "You can do it!" Rather than something like, "Gosh, you'll never get there, maybe you shouldn't try."

The single largest contributor to achieving anything I have ever described as personal success is shutting down the negative self-talk and turning on my inner cheerleader. You can, too. Let me show you how.

First, I think we have to start with why. Why do you think the things you do? When I asked myself this question, the answer came from two places: one, my childhood, and two, society and what they think or what I think others are thinking.

Let's start with number one, my childhood. I grew up in the nineties, and we had this awful, terrible word we liked to use in middle school and then high school: *conceited.* They taught girls to play small. We could not celebrate any success we experienced individually, at least not loudly or publicly. The celebration certainly could not continue to the next day. Score a point and, help the team win, and get a high five on the field in celebration with your teammates. However, if you dare share that harrowing and fun story with too many people in the coming days, dang, you come off as conceited! Score too many goals. Now you are showing off. If you get an *A* on your test, you better hide it because if you score better than your friend, she might feel bad. Make the team; you better let everyone find out on their own because if you shared the news yourself, that would be boastful.

The suppression of accolades made the turn toward self-deprecation the obvious next step. The words came easy when you never celebrated the wins. "I suck," "My hair looks terrible," and the worst of them all, "I look fat!" came with ease. Friends praised these sentiments. They agreed with common responses or similar retorts like, "Ugh, me too!" We never thought to reply with positivity.

I look back on these high school experiences and wonder if it was just me, if today I am telling myself this story of everyone's reactions to accomplishment, or if this was the actual behavior of my friends and classmates. Celebration of our accomplishments was *out* and worrying about what other people thought was *in.* To a high school student, others casting you as a conceited young woman felt like the worst punishment imaginable.

The suppression of celebrations became my first experience with self-talk. "Don't win too much." My brain told me a story not aligned with my goals. The confusion it caused developed into a pattern of behavior that would stay with me for more than twenty years.

These instances created the building blocks of my self-talk, and recognizing where they started began to give me the tools to fight against them and to become my own biggest cheerleader.

SHUTTING DOWN NEGATIVE TALK

A few months into my new job as a baseball general manager, I attended the All-Star Game in Columbus, Ohio. For the first time in my career, I was truly the only woman in the room of a high-level meeting. In fact, my introduction to the thirty-plus team presidents and GMs came as, "Welcome to the fairer sex, Emily Jaenson. Isn't this a great example of progress? Congratulations. Welcome, Emily."

Eek. That was embarrassing. Congrats to who? All these guys for hiring a woman?

Here's where I made a decision. I could shrink back in my chair and be an observer, let them all have the floor, or I could speak up and contribute. I had earned this seat at that table and chose not to stay quiet. I participated and, through this participation, learned that these men, while they had tenure, demonstrated varying skill levels. Market dependent, skill set, and job responsibilities for their team set them apart. No one was the same. With that reasoning, my special talents would be contributing factors, too.

When I realized I had something unique to contribute, everything changed. I also saw this room full of men not holding back on sharing their accomplishments. I realized negative self-talk had not entered their minds. I needed to practice this behavior, too.

I worked to shed the identity of a conceited young woman and thought I could stand on top of all my accomplishments to make greater contributions. From that position, I could show what women can do and then do more. I could extend a hand back to lead women forward in their careers.

A woman who serves in this capacity doesn't stay quiet when she earns the seat. She shows up and makes noise.

KNOWING YOUR SPECIAL TALENT

Later the next year, I participated in GM meetings in Napa Valley, California. With another year of experience under my belt, I had spent two seasons at my post and attended lots of meetings across the country. I was a quick learner and asked a lot of questions along the way from those who were further along than me. They were willing to share when I approached them with humility, clarity of ask, and feedback on their advice.

We sat in a conference room at the Marriott. Not a seat had changed since my inaugural All-Star meeting, and they had not welcomed anyone new to the fold. We had a robust agenda and one that included technology from ticket sales to team marketing. In the past year and a half, I learned I could make a great contribution to marketing. When I looked around the room and heard contributions from other leaders about marketing, their comments consisted of "Someone does that for us." The meeting leaders even passed out handouts that included basic marketing definitions like "SEO—Search Engine Optimization: the process of making your site better for search engines." This basic information was second nature to me because it was an area of continued study and curiosity. I knew by updating our marketing processes, departing from the mentality of "If it ain't broke, don't fix it," we could sell more tickets and better connect with our fans. At this moment, I truly gained clarity. We all have our special skill sets. Just because I had not been at this table for twenty years did not mean I couldn't contribute.

Any negative self-talk that crept in to tell me I didn't belong dissipated with the knowledge that I had a talent to employ. I deserved a seat at the table.

When it comes to your own self-talk, eliminate negative thoughts:

1. Identify where it is coming from. What is the origin of that negative voice? Gaining an understanding of where this all started will help you with several things, including how to identify what's happening before it can derail your goal. Acknowledge it with an "Oh yeah, I remember you and where you come from, but you can step aside while the 'me of today' works on completing this huge personal accomplishment!"

2. When you tell yourself, "They are better than me. Why even try?" Answer with, "So what?" Seriously, so what? Can you work hard and gain that experience? Can you employ your newcomer knowledge in a way that is helpful? Often, when people are in a job for a long time, they can't see what's right in front of them, and they need new eyes. That can be you. Embrace the newness. You are in the arena. You are doing the thing you have wanted to do. Like a baby deer, stand up on those wobbling legs and start to walk forward.

3. If you tell yourself, "They know more than me, and they will think I am dumb," remember grade school when teachers constantly told you there were no dumb questions. When did we forget that? Ask away. People like to share their knowledge if you ask in the right way. Consider how you would want someone to ask you for help if you were a senior and then step into those shoes. We have the opportunity to be lifelong learners. What a privilege.

4. Consider if you tell yourself, "I'm scared. I can't do it. Who am I to try because so many other people are doing this same thing, and they are definitely better than me." This voice is fear. You are trying something new and are scared. Your brain likes to stay nice and chill in its comfort zone, but you know deep down, growth never happens there. Fight the fear. Shout out, "Good for you for trying something new!" Envision the future pro who never gave up and is so proud of the younger version of yourself who had the power to stand up and keep trying. Your confidence will come as you develop your skill, and, wow, it's an incredible feeling you only get after you try.

5. What if you tell yourself, "This is too hard," "Other people can do it better," "You are an amateur," "You'll never get there," and an assortment of other demeaning phrases? You'd never say these to a friend, but these are somehow okay to tell yourself. You can be such a jerk! However, here's the thing: you really don't have to believe every stupid thing you think. That's powerful.

I've learned to practice humility instead of shrinking and confidence instead of conceit. There's a difference. I found it through purpose and changing the dialog in my head. You can, too.

We don't win all the time. A voice shows up when you are already in the arena, and things are not going your way. You are fighting your best fight, and you get a big, huge, *no*. Someone or some company says, "No. I don't want your product, I can't buy that now, or it's not for me." Somehow, though, we turn it into one of these:

- "I don't want you."
- "I'll never want you, you are terrible at your job, or how did you even get hired."
- "This is the worst product imaginable. How can you charge that price or even still be in business."

It's a horrible spiral of inner dialog, but you must pull yourself out!

First, it's not about you. Yes, business is personal because we spend so much of our time, energy, and talent on our work, and we care about our performance, income, and outcomes.

But, at the end of the day, there is the creation of a balance sheet in Excel, which makes decisions based on numbers, not on people. It is not about you, really.

Second, you earned it. Whatever role they hired you for, remember, they picked you. So, show up and do that job to the best of your abilities. Be curious when you don't know the answer. Celebrate your success so you can reinforce those behaviors. Hurdles and pitfalls will always exist, and the *you* on the other side of that hurdle is better and more experienced. Take your lows and know the highs will come if you keep working.

Third, have a good team. When you are down, tell someone. If you work on a sales team, tell your boss when you get a "no." If you are the boss, phone a friend who is in a similar role. They will tell you this: Everyone gets a no. Everyone. It's what you do afterward that counts. Business is a numbers game, and you must keep playing to get the results you want. The game is more fun with teammates, so have a crew around you to share the highs and lows. Your inner critic will go quiet when your external cheerleaders are there to pick you up.

I've been in sales in one form or another for most of my career, and I have been told "no" at least sixty-seven percent of the time. I had a thirty-three percent closing percentage when it came to sponsorship—a decent number. What it has allowed me to do is work for yes and work for no. When I get a yes, I celebrate. When I get a no, I move on and make a new outreach. I evaluate what might have gone wrong and learn from my mistakes.

Vera Quinn, CEO of Cydcor, a nine-figure outsource sales company, has this to say, "Don't take it personally. Some people are going to say no to you. It is no big deal. If I talk to ten people and nine people say no to me, that's ok! How do I go back? How do I think about my talk track? How do I think about my objection turning? It's just learning. Everything is just information. Again, when the challenge comes and sales are challenging, just step in! Don't step out."[1]

I had one prospect whom I met with at their business, then at the ballpark where they picked out their sign. Three follow-up calls later, they asked for a contract. Then, they never signed. I was infinitely annoyed and irritated and wondered what I missed. I was down on myself. My personal sales numbers, our team's sales numbers, and my commission were riding on this deal. In fact, if they had signed the contract, our team would have made our annual budget. Even though I had successfully sold multiple sponsorships that season, the old habits of negative self-talk crept in. How easy it was for me to forget all my success and focus on the negative.

With my experience and reflection on what went right, I could move past this loss with greater ease and a zero-impact hit to my confidence. I didn't get down on myself. I talked to my team, let them encourage me, and got back out there to find a new partner to sell. I realized it was not about me; this client could have dropped out for many reasons, and I would be doing myself a disservice if I created a story where I was the center, the reason they didn't buy.

Sales is a numbers game, and understanding that helps me not to take it personally when I work really hard on a proposal, have four meetings, the client drags it out for months, and then finally says "no." I have felt heartbreak when my efforts did not reach the end result I was working toward. When I look at it from a business perspective, I know it's not me. It's the way business works.

A MESSAGE FROM THE EXPERT

Vasavi Kumar is an expert in self-talk and a first-generation Indian immigrant. She grew up in a traditional Hindu household on Long Island, New York. Living and going to school in a predominantly all-white town, she struggled with figuring out her own unique identity because of the mental heartache of bullying due to her differences, her strict upbringing, and her family's focus on academics over everything. Back then, she longed for acceptance and believed she had to dumb herself down to fit in to receive a welcome into social circles.

Today, as a licensed therapist, speaker, and podcast host, she shares her tips on the *Say It Out Loud* podcast and her book of the same title. She teaches readers and listeners how to offer compassion, creativity, and acceptance to painful inner narratives.

Vasavi says, "We talk to ourselves all the time without really paying attention to what we're saying. Most of what we tell ourselves is negative, unhelpful, counterproductive, and straight-up abusive. How many times have you caught yourself telling yourself that you're stupid, incompetent, or not worthy?"[2]

Her advice is simple. Say it out loud. When you take the time to say, hear, and question what you have been telling yourself, you'll realize most of what you *know* about yourself is untrue. It's passed down from family, peers, society, media, and our cultural upbringing.[3]

In the exercise of acknowledging that unhelpful inner voice, you can change the conversation your inner self-talk is bringing to your awareness. Change the conversation to a helpful, supportive, and productive acceleration of your goals. It's amazing what happens when you start paying attention and combating that voice with intention.

Over time, as you gain skill and confidence, the voice in your head will go quiet and calm. You can train it to be supportive by celebrating your success, talking yourself up, shutting down the negative beliefs, and leveling up your skill set.

It takes practice and repetition. Start today. Your future self will be eternally grateful to the younger you.

TOP FOUR TAKEAWAYS:

1. **Recognize and challenge negative thoughts:** Become aware of any negative self-talk patterns or beliefs that may be limiting your confidence. When you catch yourself thinking negatively, challenge those thoughts by asking yourself if they are rational or if there is evidence to support them. Is what you are saying really true? Would you say that to a friend? Replace negative thoughts with positive affirmations or more realistic, constructive thoughts.

2. **Practice self-compassion:** Treat yourself with kindness and understanding, as you would treat a close friend. Acknowledge that nobody is perfect and that making mistakes or experiencing setbacks does not define your worth or competence. When a challenge arises, and it will offer yourself words of encouragement and remind yourself that failure and growth go hand in hand.

3. **Use positive affirmations:** Incorporate them into your daily routine. Repeat statements about your capabilities, strengths, and potential to reinforce positive self-beliefs. Practice saying: "I am capable and deserving of success," "I trust in my abilities to overcome obstacles," or "I am resilient and confident."

4. **Surround yourself with positive influences:** Seek out people who support and uplift you. Engage in conversations with individuals who inspire and motivate you to believe in yourself. Unfollow social media accounts that don't make you feel good. Surrounding yourself with positivity can greatly enhance your self-talk and boost your confidence.

PART III

ACTION, LET'S GO!

CHAPTER 11

Find Your People

‾‾‾‾‾

On June 24, 1999, my dad, my best friend from club soccer, her dad, and I attended a US Women's National Team Game at Soldier Field in Chicago during the 1999 FIFA Women's World Cup. It was the first time I had seen women take the field to play a professional sport, my favorite, soccer! I had been looking for female *idols* in my life who were doing big things, and this roster was full of women who could do just that.

Back then, we didn't have access to social media. It didn't exist. Our family had a 1970s version of *Encyclopedia Britannica* in the living room (any time I used these books for my homework, I had to cite the year because the information was outdated!) and dial-up internet on the home, shared computer in the basement. My phone had a cord that reached all the way to the coat closet for private conversations away from the kitchen audience of my entire family. No cell phones to text a friend, influencers to follow on social media, or lightning-fast internet to search a topic or a person on a whim.

Access to mentorship was a foreign concept to me in my small town. I didn't have access to any women working in an industry I was interested in pursuing. The bustling city of Chicago, nearly ninety minutes away from my childhood home, was a rarity for my family to visit. However, witnessing the Women's National Soccer Team step onto the field was a pivotal moment in my life. Observing these talented women playing a sport I competed in and loved in the presence of an electrifying crowd of thousands on a professional football field (a venue used by the National Football League's Chicago Bears games each season), propelled my belief in the endless potential of women. As the game concluded with a score of seven-one in favor of the US against Nigeria, I departed with a newfound roster of awe-inspiring role models.

As I continued playing soccer through high school, I eagerly anticipated the arrival of *Sports Illustrated* magazines, immersing myself in the stories and updates. It was a moment of inspiration when one of my heroes graced the cover, shedding light on her remarkable career as a professional athlete. Yet, reading the stories of their work on the field, a void remained in my understanding of life beyond the game.

In my senior year of college, I gave up playing club soccer and found inspiration from my peers who were working toward their careers post-undergraduate. I entered the realm of building my own career and felt a bit aimless. The absence of influential female figures to emulate, seek guidance from, or lean on became glaringly apparent. At twenty-one, when I had landed a *dream job* with the Chicago Bulls, I found myself navigating the city of Chicago alone, equipped only with my flawed judgment and too many missteps to count.

After leaving the Bulls and taking a new job, without recognizing the fact, I found my first mentor with my female boss, Sarah, at the Muscular Dystrophy Association in Chicago. She modeled hard work and passion and was patient to teach me how to do the job. I looked at her as a boss more than as a mentor, but reflecting all these years later, I know her leadership helped to set me on the right path in my career. She taught me how to show up for work, take my job seriously, track excellent results, and win new business.

For years following, I worked for men who served as both boss and mentor, whether they knew it or not. I learned what to do and what not to do. I had an attitude of curiosity, not monkey see, monkey do. I had a chance to watch what worked and what didn't and develop emotional intelligence by paying close attention to the environment around me. I think I did all this because I was on an island, often the only woman in the room with my only chance to grow created by observation.

I had a second influential female boss in my early thirties. Janis was like no woman I had ever seen. She was equally powerful and motherly. Her people skills were unmatched. She smothered me in her *can-do attitude* while simultaneously holding me accountable with the toughest of attitudes when I didn't pull through to her expectations. I wanted to work harder, not to fall short. I knew, as a single mother, she raised four children who were now adults, traveled the world making deals, became a grandmother, and racked up awards for her city based on the events she secured and executed flawlessly with the help of a faithful team.

While she may not have signed up to have coffee with me once a month, she was my mentor. I worked for her diligently and continued to follow her career, watching her drive down the highway to success in the carpool lane. We can't do it alone, and she taught me how to manage a good, trusted team and hold them accountable with equal toughness and love.

In Houston, I learned of a women's group for my industry through my employer and joined right away. I found commonality. Ten years into their careers, women were all dealing with the same things. The never-ending juggle of work-life balance, wanting to go for more in our careers, making it, then wondering what's next.

The twenty-somethings around me wondered if they had made the right choices if they'd ever make more money, and if they were receiving fair treatment. I began to see I was not alone. I saw a need for support for myself and women like me. We needed a trusted space to share our voices and find a connection.

It took me six months to stand on my feet in a lead role in the Minor League Baseball industry, and when I got to the top, I quickly identified that I didn't want to be standing there alone. I found friends, women who worked in the sport too and called them to make a deeper connection. Text message chains became our way to connect as we cheered each other on. We created a different environment than the one before us, where women would pull up the ladder behind them.

Internal programming can give you a running start if you are lucky enough to have it. The baseball industry did a great job with its Women in Baseball initiative. This started as an event at our annual industry meetings and turned into a monthly mentorship program. When they asked for my involvement, I quickly filled out the Google form to make myself available for mentorship, and they matched me, along with a whopping seventy-five other pairs, with a mentee. Our program featured guidelines for monthly connections plus a monthly all-participant call where we could discuss topics as a group led by a peer.

Today, many women's resource groups exist where mentors and colleagues inside or outside your place of work are ready to connect. Search "women's resource groups" and enter your industry. Talk to HR and see if you can find recommendations. Does your city, your industry, or your company offer any programs where you could get involved? Employee Resource Groups, industry chapters, of your Chamber of Commerce? You can't wait for a mentor or circle of support to fall in your lap, but you must put yourself out there and work for it. If you can't find a group right away, look for a guiding star voice through podcasts, Instagram, or blogs. Find a voice that can help you realize your full potential.

It can be intimidating to forge new connections, especially with women. We can be our own worst enemy. This comes from historically working our way to the top alone in a very competitive landscape. We have learned to compete rather than support. I did my best to stop allowing other women to intimidate me and start supporting them. What if I was just kind and helpful? What if I just asked some good questions? Could I form a relationship? I found out that the feeling of intimidation was another thing we shared in common.

Confidence comes when we cheer other people on rather than feeling threatened by them. Remember, the only person you compete with is yourself!

Today, I have found myself in networking groups, text chains, and on Zoom calls with other women. We have work to do on serious issues like the wage gap and have not yet discovered the answer to work-life balance, but our connection serves us individually and collectively. In these groups we have discussed how we each have navigated difficult situations in the workplace, asked for raises, took maternity leave, moved, and started new jobs. We have found fellowship.

Being alone in your career and buying into the thought "It's lonely at the top," is a self-fulfilling prophecy. You have to put yourself out there and make yourself available to find a buddy.

Jessica Berman, formerly Deputy Commissioner and EVP of Business Affairs at the National Lacrosse League and current Commissioner of the National Women's Soccer League, shared important insights on networks in her interview on the *Leadership is Female* podcast. When they hired her in 2019 by the National Lacrosse League, she became the first female Deputy Commissioner of a men's professional sports league. In our conversation on the podcast, Jessica says, "There is nothing more important than your relationships. I'm not sure I have always been the smartest. There might be other candidates with a better pedigree, but I feel my best asset is my relationships and network of professional colleagues. This network is so important for so many reasons—feedback and guidance. There is nothing more important than to be able to lean on those who have been in your life and whose input you'd genuinely like to seek. Also, understanding it has to be a two-way street."[1]

Jessica goes on to discuss how many of these relationships have propelled her forward and motivated her to give back. The engine of her network is full circle, utilizing the relationships she has today for advice and connection while working with those earlier in their careers to fuel a whole new line of professionals in her industry.

Jessica advised, "Put in the effort and spend the time catching up with them. Show up for people, not just when you need something from them. If someone asks you to mentor, find the time to pour into others. Make the time to give back."[2]

She credits being mindful along her journey with making these connections. Questions like who can help (recruiting others) or how can I help (activating your own network) have led to action inside these relationships. Being open-minded and not afraid to ask for help are also key contributors to keeping a network active.

Today, we are obsessed with mentorship. It's become a word that makes you feel one of two ways: relieved because you have a mentor or stressed because you don't. You probably aren't even sure what to do with your mentor and might feel nervous about ensuring you have a two-way relationship. Everyone will tell you to find a mentor. The problem is that mentors don't grow on trees.

Liz Gray and Aubree Curtis of Creative Artists Agency, an American talent and sports agency regarded as one of the most influential talent agencies in the world, serve as Cohead of Global Brand Consulting and Social Impact. Liz says that you need to understand the difference between mentors and sponsors, "You'll have multiple mentors in your career and personal life, but who is speaking up on your behalf in rooms you are not in? Those people who will share what you are doing and the value you are bringing are your sponsors."[3]

They credit their success to their network full of sponsors and mentors and their philosophy to *share the shine* and celebrate the success of others. Aubree states that, "My leadership style is to give the best to other people. Give them opportunities and find ways not to center myself always in conversations and opportunities. Share the shine. Leadership is not a singular thing; it's very intersectional at different parts of your career."[4]

As the host of the *Leadership is Female* podcast, I'll tell you that *every single woman*, powerful woman, has offered to take a call, email, or lend advice to any listener who reaches out. The network is not intimidating. It is one of service, gratitude, and helping hands. We no longer pull the ladder up behind us; we extend a hand back to lead other women forward.

The Handshake Blog, a website that calls itself the number one way for college students to find jobs, offers this advice when searching for applicable mentors. It doesn't matter whether you are twenty-two and graduating or fifty-five and searching for connection and guidance. This advice is useful!

1. Ask yourself, what are your aspirations? Put pen to paper and write down your dreams of where you'd like your career to take you.
2. What are your questions for a mentor? Write down five to seven questions that can help you clarify what you want and how you'd like to spend your time with them.
3. What kind of person do you want to learn from, and how can they best provide guidance? Is it their career, how they navigated a hurdle or made a transition to a new industry?
4. Who is currently in your network, and are any of them a good fit? Can any of those individuals introduce you to a potential mentor?
5. Who can you ask for introductions? Never underestimate the power of social media to make connections, especially LinkedIn. Look for alumni of not only your school but any volunteer organizations you have been a part of. What about people with whom you share former employment? Make an outreach. Warm intros are even better. Who knows who you want to know?
6. Once you have identified some people you'd like to connect with, it's time to ask. Call, email, or find a way to meet in person. Make sure you've done your research and approach the relationship with realistic expectations.
7. It's tough to build a relationship with someone you don't know, so find common ground. LinkedIn is great for this to see what programs they volunteer with, who their connections are, or what their alma mater is. Make it about them first. The *you* part will come. [5]

Note: I say yes to a lot of outreaches, but the ones I most commonly say no to are: "Can I pick your brain?" And "Do you have an hour where we can connect?" If you ask to pick my brain, I am assuming you don't have a specific question and have not done your research. Asking for an hour is a lot. Most busy professionals will not have an entire hour to give you, so start with something more realistic, like fifteen minutes or, if they are in town, "Can I buy you a coffee?" Better yet, if you offer to buy a coffee, bring it to their office for the fifteen minutes!

Mentors, sponsors, boards of directors, and circles of influence are all different names for the same thing: a healthy network. Don't go it alone. A mentor with substantial workplace experience can play an instrumental role in fostering personal growth and building confidence by offering insights, networking opportunities, accountability, feedback, and emotional support. Find your people, stay curious, learn from them, be vulnerable, and offer to help them, too. No one at the top got there alone, and most find success because of their willingness to connect. Join in.

TOP FOUR TAKEAWAYS:

1. **Experience and guidance:** A mentor can offer valuable insights and guidance based on their personal and professional journey. They have likely faced similar challenges and can provide practical advice on how to overcome obstacles and achieve personal growth. There is comfort in knowing you are not alone! Their wisdom and expertise can help save time and effort by steering you in the right direction and encouraging you (and cheering you on!) to push through difficult situations.

2. **Networking opportunities:** Mentors often have extensive networks built over many years in the workplace. By connecting with their mentees, they can open up doors to new opportunities and introductions. This networking can be crucial for personal growth, as it allows individuals to meet influential people, learn from their experiences, and gain exposure to different perspectives and knowledge.

3. **Accountability and feedback:** A mentor can serve as a source of accountability and provide constructive feedback. She can help identify areas for improvement, challenge limiting beliefs, and push the mentee to step out of their comfort zone. With the guidance of mentors, individuals can gain confidence in their abilities and work toward their personal growth goals with a clear roadmap by being open to feedback from a trusted source.

4. **Emotional support:** Personal growth and self-confidence are deeply rooted in emotional well-being. A mentor can provide emotional support and act as a sounding board during challenging times. Their presence can provide reassurance, validation, and encouragement, helping individuals maintain confidence in their abilities and persevere through difficult situations.

CHAPTER 12

Set Your Goals

———

When I started college at newly eighteen, the idea of finishing my degree in four years seemed insurmountable. What was my diploma even going to say? I had no clue. I applied to the University of Illinois early on the advice of my counselor, Mrs. Varney, who told me I'd get in if I did the application by the early deadline. I sat in her office with the form, and she helped me fill it out. Thank goodness she saw potential in me because although I was acing my classes and excelling in sports, I was completely lost when it came to who I was or what on earth I wanted to do with my life after the structure of high school ended.

"What do you want to study?" she asked.

"What are the choices? I have a choice? Wait, is this the 'What do you want to be when you grow up conversation?'"

I just assumed college was an extension of high school with the curriculum mapped out for me. I thought I'd have a counselor like Mrs. Varney to help me choose my next steps based on my skills. Presumably, after two years, I'd decide what was next. To my horror, I needed to decide on a college major in the fall of my senior year. This decision would set my university curriculum.

I picked pre-physical therapy. I chose this major because I thought I'd become a trainer for a professional sports team like the ones I saw running out on the football field every Sunday during an injury on the NFL field. It was my only exposure to working in sports. I received admission to Illinois, a huge feat, and dove into the unknown of this science-backed major.

Enter failure. I was barely a month into college and already backpedaling.

Two weeks into chemistry, I was already over my head. Lab had me flustered, and class was a new level of hard. I wondered if I actually liked science. I met with a person who was my college counselor. I had positive flashbacks of that meeting with Mrs. Varney and hoped this new person would help keep me going. She told me my best option might be to drop CHEM, though it would put my credit hours down to barely a full-time student, and I'd enter the no man's land of the *undecided* major. I decided to take my chances as a twelve-hour student and figure out what to do next.

As time does, it passes. As each day passed, I showed up for one class, then another, then did my homework and took tests. I finally landed in Advertising 101 during my sophomore year and found I was interested. It felt so good to be excited about a class and feel I had a path.

It was uncomfortable, but the next right step was for me to get curious. I headed to the office of the College of Communications and asked, "How do I make this my major?" They outlined the grades I needed, the classes I should take, and when to apply. Apply? I was already a student at the University, but another application to a new college within the university was necessary.

Halfway through my sophomore year, with no safety net, I applied. I practically dropped to my knees in gratitude when I got the acceptance letter several weeks later. Thankfully, in eighteen months, I transitioned from a lost freshman to a more confident sophomore with my degree plan secured.

I went on to graduate with my four-year degree on time, achieving my best grades in the last two years of school. Once I discovered a major I enjoyed, I set my sights on graduation and a career. I had finally found a direction for which to aim.

While I had achieved a taste of success, I still had not gained total clarity on the impact of setting goals. I meandered through my early twenties, taking what I thought was the next right step to a foggy destination. My only knowledge of setting goals was that most people started off the year with a New Year's resolution. The most popular is to lose weight. None of the media I consumed discusses setting goals for a life you want to achieve. I hadn't considered the concept of goal-setting in other areas of my life other than one-offs of running one race and completing one assignment at work.

The business of *right now* and the *next job* was a constant distraction. Consuming yourself with doing the work makes it easy to lack vision and just get through the day.

Now, I understand the importance of linking the work each day *with* achieving an intentional goal.

Early losses left me seeking the next easy win rather than creating a longer-term vision. I remember answering questions like, "What is your five-year vision? What is your ten-year goal? Where do you want to be?" For someone who had only lived two decades thus far, forecasting the next one-third of my life seemed far-reaching. I know now that a vision for the future would have made the choices I had each day clearer. What if we asked about quarterly goals? Six-month goals? Annual goals? Would that make the idea of setting goals for young people easier? I think so.

THE PROCESS OF GOAL-SETTING DISCOVERED

While in my thirties, I developed a process to set goals for my life, and I'd like to share it with you. No matter our age, setting goals for ourselves can lead us on a journey of self-discovery and empowerment. When we focus on achieving milestones, are clear with our intentions, and don't let challenges block our progress, we will lead a purposeful life, building confidence by working toward each achievement. Set goals today. Imagine what you could achieve with a clear annual vision and goals.

Having a desire but no plan on how to work toward its achievement accomplishes nothing. What's worse than not having a plan to achieve goals is not thinking big enough in the first place. Many people get stuck in their comfort zones and won't think big enough to work toward a greater accomplishment. That's why we need to set personal and professional goals for ourselves and have a plan to get there. We've traveled further and learned more than if we never tried at all, even if we fall short. Let's live a big life. Let's set goals.

According to a 2023 Gallup poll, "Seven in ten US adults are poised to set goals for themselves at the start of a new year, with one-third telling Gallup they are 'very likely' to do so and another 38 percent 'somewhat likely.'"[1] When you look deeper, only a third of goal-setting intenders plan to take the three key steps to reach their objectives. In deeper review, can we really count on 'somewhat likely' as goal-getting? If people are wishy-washy on even making a commitment to set goals, will they? Unlikely.

Take these proven steps to set and reach your goals:

1. Write them down.
2. Make a detailed plan for reaching them.
3. Focus on your goals throughout the year.

I applied this process when running my first marathon. I used the goal-setting exercise we will dive into below to identify my goal: complete a marathon. I discovered a detailed plan by using an application, RunKeeper, to outline a detailed marathon plan. The plan contained the weekly training necessary to reach my goal day by day. If I stuck to the plan,

I'd complete the race. The three steps worked; I accomplished my goal when I crossed the finish line and received my medal.

In an article published by *Inc* magazine, a new study showed that by implementing the last step above and focusing on you goals throughout the year, you can experience a thirty-three percent greater success rate. In addition to the three steps outlined above, they added two additional steps. The first additional step, build high levels of accountability by telling someone about your goals. This improved performance significantly. Finally, "To generate the desired outcome, add one important step: Write a weekly progress report and send it to the person they talked to about their goals."[2] Checking on progress frequently, with accountability from a coach or friend, increases the likelihood that you will succeed.

If you are not feeling motivated yet, in Jeff Boss's article for *Forbes*, he gives us five reasons to set goals that will help create your Why for this activity.[3]

1. Goals trigger behavior. Having a clear, compelling goal mobilizes your focus toward actionable behavior. Goal setting should motivate you. What will be your end result when you reach your goal? Envision yourself embracing that win and create a mental cue to trigger your focus and motivate you to get to work.

2. Goals guide your focus. When you set a goal, you naturally direct your attention toward the next step and, as a result, lead yourself in the right direction, which forces your actions—your behaviors—to follow. The body follows the mind.

3. Goals sustain momentum. Seeing progress is addictive because of the dopamine released in your brain after attaining a reward. You've pushed your comfort zone just a little further. Your brain agrees you've been successful and rewards you with a great feeling. That will create momentum.

4. Goals align your focus. Goal setting helps you align focus with behavior because you get feedback on your progress. The actions you take—or avoid—offer clues about your values, beliefs, challenges, strengths, and weaknesses, which allow you to course correct as necessary and reset your goal achievement strategy (and subsequently, your focus).

5. Goal setting promotes self-mastery. Goals work because they build character. While the process of goal setting is important because it helps unearth and identify what's truly important to you, pursuing your goals is the real money-maker (literally and figuratively) because it builds self-efficacy. It develops you as the type of person who *can* achieve goals.

LET'S SET YOUR GOALS

Given all this research, I hope we are all on the same page that goal setting is essential for increasing your confidence and attaining new levels of achievement in your life. An exercise I like to use to set goals gives you a running start: reflection on the past year's accomplishments. Goal-setting provides an opportunity for self-reflection and personal growth.

As you reflect on your progress, you become more self-aware and develop a deeper understanding of your strengths and weaknesses. This process of self-discovery is vital in building confidence because it allows you to appreciate your development over time, identify areas for improvement, and celebrate the progress you have made thus far.

ASK YOURSELF THESE QUESTIONS:
1. What was your biggest professional achievement of the prior year?
2. What was your biggest personal achievement of the prior year?
3. What was the most important lesson you learned in business the prior year?
4. What was the most important lesson you learned in your personal life in the prior year?
5. What felt difficult one year ago in your work that feels easier today?
6. What felt difficult one year ago in your personal life that feels easier today?

Now, you have a running start to set your goals for the next year because you know how far you've already come.

FOR YOUR NEXT YEAR, ANSWER THESE:
1. What are three things you hope to improve upon in business the next year?
2. What are three things you hope to improve upon in your personal life in the next year?
3. What do you want to spend more time on professionally in the next year? What do you enjoy in your job that you

hope to do more of? List the top three things you want to achieve professionally.

4. What do you want to spend more time on personally in 2023? What do you enjoy outside of work that you want to do more of? List the top three things you want to achieve personally.

If we are going to dream big, let's get extra credit. Stretch yourself. Dream bigger or use this section to plug in smaller goals that you need to keep at the forefront of your brain to continue down the path of success you are already traveling. Don't miss the chance to earn extra credit in your life.

DEFINE TWO GOALS IN EACH OF THESE FOUR CATEGORIES.

Challenge: What would be a big challenge for you? What would stretch you beyond what you think you are capable of? Write down two challenges for yourself here.

Achieve: What would be meaningful for you to achieve? An industry award? Win a spot on the school PTO? A racing medal? Finish writing a book and achieve the title of author? A raise? A title promotion? Name it and call your shot.

Learn: What will you learn this year? Will you take an online course? Read a certain number of books? Enroll in college? Your masters? Up-skill in your job?

Health: How will you take care of your health this year? Sleep eight hours a night, drink at least half your body weight in ounces of water daily, enroll at a new gym, meditate five times a week, and take cold showers? What two goals will you define to improve your health this year?

Defining two or three in each area is intentional. We don't achieve a laundry list. It's simply too much. Identifying areas of focus and delineating between work and home gives you guardrails for your goals and helps you work on your whole self. Imagine if you completed everything on your goal list: Incredible progress in one year. Imagine if you completed half? Still incredible progress! Most of us are guilty of proclaiming how fast a year can go by; imagine the feeling of having an intentional year focused on growth. That's what I call a celebratory toast on NYE and the way to enter the new year on fire.

What's the next right thing you can do to reach your goal? Think about your future self. Who are you in one month, one year? Taking the next right step in pursuing your goals puts you on a path to the person you want to become. You exchange comfort for discomfort and well, it's uncomfortable but if you believe in yourself and build the willpower to take the next right step you'll look back and won't believe how far you've gone.

WAIT, THERE IS MORE!

While goal setting is a large part of the equation, you must also confront your fears so you are brave enough to take your first action step toward reaching your goals.

Tim Ferriss encourages us in his TEDx Talk to define our fears, too. The hard choices—what we most fear doing, asking, and saying—are very often exactly what we need to do. How can we overcome self-paralysis and take action? Mr. Ferris encourages us to fully envision and write down our fears in detail in a simple but powerful exercise he calls *fear-setting*.[4]

You should feel incredible momentum from setting your goals. Your dreams are soaring!

Consider this, though: When you are going after a new challenge, it's reasonable to think a feeling of fear will creep in as you enter a new territory. Once you've set your goals wearing rose-colored glasses and thinking about how you'll celebrate when you succeed, you face the day-one realities that you've never been here before. Even if you have, you quit.

So, what do you do?

This practice of fear setting can help you thrive in high-stress environments. The new territory of step-by-step going after your goals, separating what you can control from what you cannot. The phrase "what if" is paralyzing. *What if I fail? What if I fail publicly? What will they think? What if I can't do it? Then what?*

According to Ferris, "The recommendation is to start by defining your fear. Call it out. Define all the what-ifs. Decide how you might prevent them. And, if they happen, how will you repair these pitfalls?"[5]

The final ingredient to successfully setting your goals is to simply define your fears, determine how you will prevent your fear from stopping your progress, and, if fear does get in the way, think of how you will repair the damage and continue your progress.

Use the goal-setting exercise to have your next best year. Call your dang shot. Use the confidence you are building to empower yourself to take the next right step. Before you get too far, take a second to define your fears. If you call it out, those fears can't hide in the dark, jump out, and scare you so badly that you stop. If you know where the fear is hiding and you have a plan to get through it, you'll have a much higher chance of achieving your goals.

Keep moving forward. You deserve to live the life of your dreams, and you can't let a shortsighted vision or a pitfall knock you down. Stay the path. Through clarity and focus, achieving milestones, overcoming challenges, and reflecting on personal growth, you embark on an exhilarating journey of self-discovery and empowerment. So, I encourage you to craft your goals, take charge of your destiny, and witness the transformational power it has in enhancing your confidence, enabling you to lead a purposeful life. Let's go!

TOP FOUR TAKEAWAYS:

1. **Clarity and focus.** When you set clear goals for yourself, it helps crystalize your vision and direction in life. Once you know what exactly you want to achieve, you become more focused on taking the necessary steps toward reaching your goal. Focus eliminates ambiguity and instills a sense of purpose, enabling you to build confidence in your abilities to navigate the path ahead.

2. **Achieving milestones.** Setting achievable goals allows you to experience a series of small victories that contribute to your overall growth and success. Each milestone of accomplishment reinforces your belief in your capabilities and reminds you that progress is attainable. With every mini-triumph, your confidence grows, forming a solid foundation for advancing toward more ambitious aspirations.

3. **Overcoming challenges.** Setting goals challenges you to step outside your comfort zone and confront obstacles head-on. As you encounter setbacks or roadblocks along your journey, you learn valuable lessons about resilience, adaptability, and problem-solving. Overcoming challenges, even if they seem insurmountable at times, builds grit and mental fortitude, strengthening your confidence in your ability to conquer future obstacles.

4. **Reflecting on personal growth.** Goal-setting provides an opportunity for self-reflection and personal growth. As you continually evaluate your progress and adjust your goals, you become more self-aware and develop a deeper understanding of your strengths and weaknesses. This process of self-discovery is vital in building confidence because it allows you to appreciate your development over time, identify areas for improvement, and celebrate the progress you have made thus far.

CHAPTER 13

Increase Your Confidence

―――

A text came in from my old colleague, Chris, "You should apply to speak at TEDx." The words accompanied a screenshot of the press release from TEDxReno, a notoriously great event that produced high-quality talks for the TEDx YouTube channel, where a few of the past speakers had racked up millions of views.

I considered what topic I might present. I reflected on all that had happened in the last several years in my leadership positions and the growth I had experienced since my childhood growing up in a small town in Illinois. Add in the over one hundred interviews I had recorded with female leaders in business on my *Leadership is Female* podcast and the lessons my guests and I had shared with the world, and I had an idea. I thought I'd talk about the concept of "finding your voice," one of the most discussed topics regarding hockey stick curve career growth. Then I wondered, what proceeded the "finding your voice" breakthrough? You first need to grow the confidence to use your voice.

In the last twenty years, day by day, I developed my confidence skill set. I could use the confidence I had developed and tell the story about how listeners could use the behaviors I had learned since high school to change their attitude from "too shy to order a pizza" to one of greater confidence over time.

I didn't have all my thoughts developed, but I knew I needed to present on this topic. From the interviews I did on my podcast, I heard a recurring theme: increasing one's confidence had been a major part of the breakthrough to reach new career heights. The questions, *What if we had more confidence?* and *What could we achieve if we weren't so afraid to try?* rang in my head. Many intelligent people on this planet have unlimited potential, but their own self-doubt has stood in their way. It was time to go after my next opportunity. I opened my computer and submitted my application.

Weeks later, I got a call from the TEDx event director. He explained he had received hundreds of applicants. Many from around the country. I had made the top ninety, then seventy, then thirty. Ultimately, he selected me as one of the top twenty to participate in TEDxReno 2022 with one caveat. I first had to defend my talk. He reminded me TED had an entire channel dedicated to confidence, so what was it I would say that would make my talk unique and different?

I replied, "Bret, have you ever visited the creamer aisle at the grocery store?"

Perplexed, he answered, "Yes."

"There are unlimited flavors—even seasonal—vanilla, sweet cream, caramel, gingerbread, pumpkin spice... then different types of milk, full fat, fat-free, almond, oat. There is something for everyone. I believe that's similar to the message about confidence. It depends on who you hear it from, how they tell the story, and where the listener is at in their life that makes a talk resonate. I believe my talk will have the right flavor for a certain audience and resonate differently than what has already been posted. Give me a shot."

I had him sold. This type of storytelling was what he and the audience would have to look forward to on event day. Ending our conversation, I expanded on a few ideas, and I was in!

I shared the news with my friend Chris, and he texted this reply, "That's terrific! I'll let them share my 'Emily' with the universe. I can't wait to hear you." Followed by a bunch of emojis with fire, muscles, and sunglasses.

They were going to record me on stage delivering a talk to thousands in the room, and if all went well, millions on YouTube. I knew the only way to do my best was to remain disciplined to master my delivery and, in the event director's words, "To create the best short talk of my life."

The process of idea to stage was interesting, and if you remain open to feedback, it is one that will create an incredible talk. It consisted of three rounds. First, you read version one to the entire committee. Thirty evaluators monitored my speech. After I concluded my read, one by one, they went around the room to tell me what they liked and what they didn't. My head spun when the organizer gave the final comments.

I left the room, headed home, and jotted down what I could remember. I let the feedback sit for a week before I revisited my writing. I made the changes and went in for round two a month later. This time, ten professionals evaluated my talk, and we did the same process. We ended with the lead organizer, Bret, who was harsh. He didn't like the changes. He was worried it was not coming together. I had a strange feeling wash over me that felt like embarrassment. My improvement between rounds seemed to slide backward instead of forward. I trusted I could deliver a great talk but needed to take into greater consideration the feedback from the group and be confident that my talk on confidence could deliver.

I leaned into the suggestions… except for one. The suggestion was to research the topic through other TEDx Talks. That would not work for me. I didn't want their work to color what I was performing or to unintentionally become a parrot of another's work.

I worked hard to improve it and emailed Bret to let him know I would not be available in person for round three. He emailed a reply, "Call me. Normally, this is a disqualifier."

I had to go to battle again. I knew in my bones that what I had to say would resonate, and my talk on confidence would inspire many to know that if they worked at it, they could develop a more confident attitude.

With some additional arm twisting, Bret agreed to meet over Zoom. I read my final version to an emotionless Bret. At the conclusion, he exhaled and said, "Wow, that is good. I must admit I was very worried after your second presentation, but now I see it came together and is going to be great. Go practice."

I recorded myself reading my speech, and for two weeks, I listened to that speech in my car over and over again, trying to get myself to a point where I could talk along with the recording.

The week before the talk, in my house, I practiced for an hour at the beginning of the day, holding my speech in my hand and pacing around my closet. In the afternoon, I'd pace around my office, reciting the speech aloud, waving my arm with one hand and tightly gripping the papers in another.

Thursday before TEDx, I advanced to a rehearsal with the talk on my desk, only referencing the paper at a few key sticking points. On Friday, a friend generously offered her State Farm staff as a sounding board, and I performed all the way to point three before I hit a wall, grabbed the paper, read from it, and got back on track to finish it out. Crap. I didn't have it memorized, and I questioned my discipline.

Afterward, I called my husband. "Great," he said. "You got the mess up out of your system. No way you are doing that tomorrow."

Friday night before TEDx, we had a speaker dinner with the sponsors. I chatted with several folks in the room who told me how nervous I should be. They said things like, "Wow, this will be hard, aren't you scared?" I remember thinking to myself this does not feel like a motivational dinner. This feels like a crawl-under-a-rock-and-hide situation. Were they trying to scare me?

A committee member wondered how my talk had progressed. She weighed in early and gave me pointers. I asked her how her talk went in a previous iteration of the event, and she replied, "Oh, I never did a talk. I have terrible stage fright!"

It was at that point when my husband grabbed my shoulders and said, "You got this. At this point, you are one of the only people brave enough to enter the arena. In my eyes, you have already won."

The day of the event was bizarre. All the speakers were so nervous. I could visibly see their legs shaking on stage during one speaker's delivery. The talk in the green room involved the word "nervous" in every sentence.

I decided my mindset would be one of excitement, celebration, and, dare I say, fun! I sequestered myself in the back room and started performing my speech with unbounded energy. I would celebrate this milestone of getting here and give the best, most confident short talk of my life.

And I did! It felt amazing. I raised my arms in celebration at the end of the talk, left the stage, and let the emotion of a few tears fall. I did it. I had fun. It went well. My identity had evolved to include a title I'd wear proudly and confidently: TEDx speaker.

After this huge build-up, I think it's only fair I share my TEDx Talk with you. It's entitled, "The Six Behaviors to Increase Your Confidence."[1]

In high school, my mom asked me to call and order pizza for the family on a Friday night. I found the number in the phone book and handed the phone to my older brother to place the order. I was too shy to talk to a stranger.

Fast forward to college at the University of Illinois, my first time away from my small town. I spent the first several weeks crying in my dorm room, too homesick to go out and partake in early freshman partying. The one frat party I attended for less than an hour was so disappointing I wanted to trade in my books, abandon my major, and move back to the comfort of my hometown.

Then, I picked up my eyes to look around at the confident people around me. These students made their way around a big campus just fine, heads held high, pursuing a degree they had chosen that would lead to them living out their dream.

And I wanted that kind of confidence, too. I wanted to pursue my dream. That's why I had chosen to go away to school in the first place. However, my behaviors did not align with these confident attitudes. Crying on my bunk bed in my dorm room, shying away from social engagement, not showing up for class because I was worried others were smarter than me... I wondered how I would get to this level of confidence necessary to live out the dreams I had set for myself. I realized what I needed was to change.

Research tells us that the way to get people to change is not to start with trying to change their attitudes alone but to start with the behaviors associated with the attitudes. When people see themselves behaving differently, they can then think of themselves differently, and the attitude change will follow. Choose to exhibit behaviors consistent with the change you want to see.

So, the questions were:

Who am I?

Who do I want to become, and how does that person behave?

My answer was that I wanted to have a successful career that meant something that allowed me to contribute and serve others. For me, that was a career as a sports executive.

To achieve this, I needed to become a more confident person, and I did. Thirteen years later, I became the first female general manager of a Triple-A baseball team in nearly twenty years.

I also went on to host the *Leadership is Female* podcast, where I have interviewed over eighty female executives in sports, an industry that's over eighty percent male at the management level and above, and time after time, confidence is the number one skill they have improved to earn their spot at the top of the sports industry.

Rising to the top of their field required each woman to go where they had not gone before requiring a confidence they, like me, had not yet acquired. When they changed their behaviors and began to act more confident, their attitude followed.

I want to share a series of *six* behaviors you can *start today* to increase your confidence. Start behaving like a confident person, and you will start seeing yourself as a confident person.

Why is it important to increase your confidence? Think of this: How would you act, or what could you *achieve* if you were to *ten times your confidence*?

#1. **Count yourself in.** I spoke to Nicki Jones, a sideline broadcaster in college sports for ESPN+, and she told me about the first time she did sideline reporting for a nationally televised game. She was shaking in her heels, standing courtside, microphone in hand under the hoop, until she heard something familiar in her headset: "We will be on in five… and three, two, one, you're live," and she performed at her best, the nerves melting away.

Nicki says, "When I hear the producer in my ear, when he's counting down until I'm live, until it's my turn, to have my hit and tell my story, he's at ten seconds, I'm nervous. At five, I'm still shaking. He gets to three, two, one, and the light bulb comes on, and I'm performing."

Nicki's an athlete, a former basketball player. She knows the game and is no stranger to working through tough situations on the court by the clock. The tactic remained true. Counting will get you started, and the momentum will keep you going.

I have used this technique. I have had to have many conversations I was dreading, but one I vividly remember was standing on the warning track of the baseball field forty-five minutes before game time, looking at the opposing Manager and his team wearing the wrong color uniform and feeling like I wanted to turn and run back up to my office. Instead, I faced him and said in my head, three, two, one, go and started walking toward him. When I arrived, I started talking, and we had a very uncomfortable conversation about his team wearing the wrong color uniform! Yes, I had to ask all these grown men to change into an opposing color. It was so awkward! But when I asked myself, who am I and how to I behave, the answer was I am a person who leads by following the rules and am not too shy to stand up for what's right and what is true to the game. Counting got me started, and momentum kept me going.

#2. **To push yourself, do something beyond what you think you are capable of, and give yourself twenty seconds of courage.** What if you only had to be brave for a total of twenty seconds? For me, this behavior enormously helped when I published my podcast, *Leadership is Female,* bold title and all, to go live for all the world to see, hear, critique, and have their opinions. I remember sitting on the carpet on my closet floor. Looking at the recording. Asking myself if I should listen to it just one more time. Does it need any more edits? Then I said aloud, Emily, give yourself twenty seconds of courage, and I hit "publish," and it was complete. And I kept breathing and the world kept turning and the podcast grew into what it was meant to be. All because of twenty seconds of courage.

#3. **Take a seat at the table**! Not metaphorically speaking; actually, take a seat at the table. I spoke with Rachel Luba, a player agent who represents some of the biggest names in baseball. She told me this story about taking a seat at the table. She noticed women waiting for the seats to fill and standing along the edges of the room, and worse yet, she was doing it, too. To become the more confident woman she envisioned herself to be, she had to start behaving like one by taking her physical seat at the table. The woman she wanted to be sat down, shared her ideas, and got the deal done. Rachel said, "I would see all these guys giving all these guys their opinions, and no one ever asked me. In the beginning, as a female, you have to be okay with speaking up. No one will ask your opinion if you are quiet, they will let you be quiet. You have to speak up when you are at the table. Assert yourself." When she began to act like herself, it was the turning point of her career with one simple action—taking a seat at the table.

#4. **Cheer someone else on**. They say women will pull up the ladder behind them. What if you didn't? What if you extended a hand back to lead her forward? What if you celebrated the success of a colleague rather than feeling sorry for yourself it was not you accepting the accolades? You take your control back when you cheer for someone's accomplishments rather than competing with them. Think of this great quote from Amy Poehler, "Good for her, not for me." It turns that pit in your stomach of "She did that, and I'm still here," on its head to make you think, yes, good for her! Not for me. This is not my celebration. It's hers. I'll cheer for her, and my time will come. And when it does, it's going to be great to have the same support I shared with others.

Wins are so much better when we celebrate together. Join in. Cheer someone else on.

Here's #4 in action: Recently, Anne Marie Gianutsos received a phone call with an offer to interview for the job of CMO of the Drone Racing League. Anne Marie said, "The current president, Rachel Jacobson, had met her ten years earlier in a networking program in New York City and kept in touch. When Rachel called her about her opportunity to become president of the Drone Racing League, Anne Marie was in her ear, hyping her up, telling her to go for it. Imagine my surprise and delight when, a couple of months later, she called to let me know she was conducting a search for a head of marketing." The offer came after Anne Marie's sincere congratulatory outreach and encouragement to the newly named female league president, Rachel. See how that works? Confident people celebrate the success of others rather than feeling threatened. Cheer for another person's success.

#5. **Grow your confidence for a new challenge through a great performance of a skill you can already perform with excellence.** What are you really good at? Ask yourself what you are most proud of and write it down. Ask yourself what is easier today than it was one year ago and write it down. The answers to these questions are where confidence is born. These answers show the growth you have experienced. You can look back and acknowledge the skills you have built over time to bolster your confidence today. Confidence is born in these moments of recognition of all you've already done and already achieved.

One woman I interviewed on the *Leadership is Female* podcast was going after a big promotion with a top team. Before she went in for her pitch to her boss, she reviewed her current job description, made notes on her accomplishments in all areas mentioned, and prepared herself with examples of her great work. She had confidence in her performance before her big meeting by reviewing all her successes. She got the promotion. Grow confidence in new areas through your already excellent performance in others.

#6. **Celebrate constantly.** Celebrate the everyday wins. How often do we reach our goals and immediately move on? When you do this, the recall of the success diminishes. Your brain's reward system can't channel your success in a healthy way to increase your confidence if you can't even remember what you have achieved or, worse, link that accomplishment to stress. Find ways to celebrate that are meaningful to you, like creating a highlight reel photo album inside your cell phone of your most proud accomplishments, taking yourself or your colleagues out for celebratory drinks after you close the big deal, getting a massage or a pizza when you reach your personal goals. It doesn't matter. Create a memory to celebrate your accomplishment. This will help your brain to rewire and reinforce the behaviors that led to the success in the first place.

I've come a long way from the girl who couldn't order a pizza to the woman who became GM of a professional minor league baseball team, started a podcast, and delivered a TEDx Talk. All because I decided to start practicing behaviors to become a more confident person. I hope you'll make that decision too. Because how many runs could you score if you were ten times more confident?

IT'S UP TO YOU

Use these six behaviors, and I can guarantee you'll find the confidence you've been looking for. I could have let my identity shift crush my confidence. Instead, I embraced a new challenge: becoming a TEDx speaker. My goal was to push myself to grow and take on something new. I set a goal: impact one person. If this talk helped just one person, it could have a ripple effect around the world. What I could have never imagined was reaching three million views in the first year and hearing from so many people around the world who took the time to let me know how my talk has helped them to increase their confidence.

Confidence can waver. However, if you use these six behaviors, I can guarantee you'll find the conviction you have been looking for. In practice, these behaviors will help you to increase your confidence over time. Trust your abilities and how far you've come. Trust that if you stay the path more opportunities will come your way.

Confidence plays a huge role in achieving our dreams. We must have the confidence to believe our dreams are possible. These behaviors will change your attitude and give you the self-assurance to grow from who you are today into who you are meant to be. Which *confident behavior* will you choose to use today?

I believe we can all make our own unique mark on this world. All it takes is your willingness to put yourself out there. Take these behaviors to reach new heights. I'm cheering for you!

TOP FOUR TAKEAWAYS:
1. **Increased self-belief:** Practicing confident behaviors can boost your self-belief, enabling you to have a positive attitude toward your goals. By consistently exuding confidence, you will start to believe in your abilities and potential to achieve what you desire.
2. **Overcoming obstacles:** Confidence is essential in facing and overcoming obstacles. When you practice confident behaviors, you develop resilience and a mindset that refuses to back down in the face of challenges. This helps you navigate through setbacks and find alternative solutions to reach your goals.
3. **Improved communication:** Confidence radiates through effective communication. By practicing confident behaviors, you start to see yourself as a more poised person. You enhance your communication skills, making it easier to articulate your thoughts and ideas. This will help you connect with others, build relationships, and gain support toward achieving your goals.
4. **Inspiring others:** Your confidence will inspire those around you. By embodying self-assurance, you become a role model, showcasing what is achievable through belief in oneself. Your confident attitude will motivate and encourage others to pursue their own goals, adding positive ripple effects to the people in your life. If you can't do it for yourself, do it for others.

CHAPTER 14

Say Yes

———

Five years before I became GM, a year after moving to Nevada, a job in Minor League Baseball came up; our city was lucky enough to have a Triple-A baseball team in town. The offer was to join the team in a low-level position in corporate partnerships, selling advertising space at the ballpark to local and national businesses. This offer was at least five years below my current experience level and half the pay I had earned in previous roles. It was not the offer I had hoped for. After exhausting all my negotiating skills and asking for a bigger title and salary, I had a conversation with my husband in the living room of our starter home about whether or not I should take the job.

I explained to him the role. He asked me if I would enjoy it. The answer was yes. He asked if it was more in line with what I wanted to do. I said yes. He asked what was holding me back, and I told him I felt like I was starting over. He reminded me I was capable of more, but I'd just have to prove it.

Following that conversation, I made a commitment to myself. I'd say yes to the job offered and commit myself to earning the role I knew I deserved. I poured in all my efforts to meet and exceed the company's goals and elevate as a leader. Two and a half years later, I was a vice president of the team.

I said yes to a lower offer than I thought I deserved because I knew it was an opportunity. I'd take a short-term loss to prove a long-term gain. I said yes to myself, confidently believing that if I put in the time and energy, I'd earn the position I thought I deserved. Often, the offers we hope for don't come perfectly packaged with our favorite color bow. They look a bit different, and it's up to us to create the perfect fit and find the opportunity created by taking the leap.

Several months following my promotion, our family chose another yes. We moved to Houston. My husband received an offer for his first corporate job following his military service, and we took a leap of faith again. I had to network in a city where I knew no one and figure out which opportunity would be best for me.

It took nearly six months to land a contract role with the Harris-County Houston Sports Authority. I accepted the role of sales director for a new event. The organization had run the NCAA Final Four earlier that year (dang, I missed it!), and the Super Bowl was on the horizon. However, in my current offer, I was only able to serve as a volunteer for the Super Bowl. These two events I had dreamed to work on full time, but the opportunity to work on the flashy events wasn't on the table. "World Corporate Games sales director" was the only role available. I said yes, even though the offer was not perfect. I felt the flexibility of the role would be good for my family, and I had a chance to work major events, which would be an enhancement to my resume after working in full-season sports for the majority of my career.

Over the next two years, I worked diligently and found some measure of success and experience in my role, added another beautiful child to our family, Anders, and built a new home nicely tucked into a Houston suburb. We had our family of four and a house we loved when another opportunity came knocking. The opportunity to return to Reno to become GM of the Minor League Baseball team I had previously worked for and climbed the ladder, the Reno Aces. I had every reason to say no. We had started a new life in Texas, had two young children, a nice salary, and a brand-new house. Who would leave that?

After a week of consideration drawn out on a poster-board-sized pros and cons list, we decided to say yes. The opportunity was too good to pass up. In this case, we'd move for my job, and my husband would need to look for work, but we would figure it out. We would bet on ourselves.

My husband and I have a motto, "You've got one life. Live the best one you can." The key to doing that is going after *more,* answering the call to *what if,* and moving toward the pursuit. It means saying yes to a new opportunity to stay in the arena and move toward a bigger, better version of ourselves.

We never know the answer to *what if.* In my case, I know if I had not taken what I had considered a lower-level job than I deserved, my path would not have led to being the first female GM of a Triple-A baseball team in nearly twenty years, my tremendous growth in confidence, a TEDx talk, a speaking career, and a person with enough to share to become a published author.

I do want to acknowledge a very real acronym, FOSY, or Fear of Saying Yes, a reality for over half of the adult population. "FOSY is a common phenomenon linked to the emotions we experience when faced with opportunities that push us outside our comfort zone," says psychologist Emma Kenny. "When there's a chance we might face judgment, or we have preconceived ideas we're not good at something, our instinctive, knee-jerk reaction is to say 'no.' The research tells it's even more common to say no to something, even if it's something we want to do."[1]

"The benefits of doing more of the things we wish we could but are afraid to say 'yes' to are vast," Kenny continues. "When we take on new experiences, we grow in courage and develop personal resilience which increases our confidence and self-esteem, making life feel altogether more rewarding."[2]

However, a study by OnePoll conducted on this fear found that even when people were scared of saying "yes," they had hope in using that answer. Thirty-six percent of respondents wanted their lives to be busier and with more variety. Forty-three percent feel having the ability to say "yes" to more will bring a sense of fulfillment. And forty percent hope it will make them a more positive person. Despite having fear, we can see yes brings opportunities. You are not alone if you are afraid. Find the will to say yes.[3]

THE "YES" APPLICATION

In 2014, Shaye Haver, a lieutenant in the US Army, discussed on the podcast her interpretation of an internal Army message stating, "The combat exclusionary clause will be lifted by the Secretary of Defense, and women would be introduced into different roles in the military. Because of the war on terror, they would be looking into what women were contributing and what they needed to do these roles better."[4]

In layman's terms, women have historically been prohibited from jobs that put them in direct combat. This message opened the door to combat positions, including elite special forces like Army Rangers.

Shaye said, "I was a brand-new lieutenant at Fort Carson when this came out, and I was getting ready to do my first gunnery." Shaye had already achieved much as an Apache helicopter pilot and a triathlete. She remembered reading the news and thinking, "Wow, that is a big deal." She then remembers saying aloud from her desk, "That is badass. Good for those girls!" Shaye didn't even consider she could be one of "those girls."[5]

Later that month, when she got ready for gunnery, General George came out to meet the unit and happened upon Shaye's platoon. They introduced Shaye as a "squared-away lieutenant who could hold her own in any PT event." General George shook Shaye's hand and said, "Do you want to go to Ranger School?"

Shaye replied, "No sir!"[6]

But General George planted a seed in Shaye's mind. Maybe Ranger School was a possibility for her.

In the coming weeks, she passed gunnery, and her battalion commander encouraged her to try Ranger School. Shaye reflected, "There are leaders out there who see things in us we don't necessarily see in ourselves. Or that we don't know we are capable of doing."[7] She took the recommendations of those two leaders and got to work preparing for the US Army Ranger School.

Shaye did pre-Ranger training, completed her order of merit list (OML), and received admission to Ranger School at the top of her class. She decided to own it, to buy in, and say yes to this opportunity. She decided to drive to Fort Benning, Georgia, and not return until she earned her Ranger tab. Five months later, she and Kristen Greist became the first two women ever to graduate from the US Army Ranger School. In 2016, she and Kristen ranked thirty-fourth on *Fortune* magazine's list of World's Greatest Leaders.[8]

HOW TO SAY YES AND HOW TO KNOW WHEN IT'S RIGHT

Shonda Rhimes, creator of one of my favorite shows and a woman I thought was invincible, did a talk on the TED stage about her "year of saying yes." She said, "The very act of doing the thing that scared me undid the fear, made it not scary. My fear of public speaking, my social anxiety, poof, gone. The power of one word is amazing. 'Yes' changed my life. 'Yes' changed me."[9]

Her talk was about saying yes to something she didn't want to do—the main reason we usually say no. The opportunity is scary. It's outside our comfort zone. We might fail... we come up with so many reasons to say "no." Through Shonda's commitment to "yes," she could reconnect with the feeling she most enjoys, the "hum" of excellence.

QUESTIONS TO ASK YOURSELF IF YOUR GUT IS TELLING YOU TO CHANGE YOUR "NO" TO A "YES":

1. Can you think of an opportunity that feels too hard or too scary to say yes?
2. Does this opportunity align with your values?
3. Does this opportunity align with your goals?
4. What is my intention in saying no to this? Is it fear-based?
5. What does my gut say? Get silent and ask yourself if no is the right answer. Ask yourself a second time. How is your body reacting? Can you feel a spark of hope, excitement, or potential? If so, your body is telling you what to do.
6. What is the opportunity? What if it all goes right?
7. Remove other people's opinions. What would I do if I knew no one would be disappointed either way?

You will find many ways to say "yes" in these examples. A yes to your destiny. A yes to an opportunity. A hell no to get to a hell yes. A yes to everything to rediscover you. Whatever tactic you choose, do it with intention. Do it with your whole heart. A yes is your commitment to show up as your whole self, give it your all, build, learn, and grow. Yes is your opportunity.

TOP FOUR TAKEAWAYS:

1. **Personal growth:** Saying yes to a challenging opportunity allows you to step out of your comfort zone and push your limits. It presents an opportunity for personal growth, teaching you to overcome obstacles, build resilience, and develop new skills that you wouldn't have acquired otherwise. Embracing difficulty can lead to transformative experiences and help you unlock your potential.

2. **Building confidence:** Taking on a challenging opportunity can be intimidating, but it can also be an incredible confidence booster. By conquering difficult tasks or situations, you prove to yourself that you are capable of achieving more than you may have initially believed. This can have a significant positive impact on your self-confidence and self-esteem, empowering you to face future challenges with resilience and conviction.

3. **Achieving success:** Many successful individuals attribute their accomplishments to taking risks and embracing challenging opportunities. Saying yes to a difficult opportunity can open doors to success that you may have otherwise missed. It allows you to demonstrate your drive, dedication, and willingness to tackle tough situations, which often leads to favorable outcomes and further opportunities for growth and advancement.

4. **Broadening perspectives:** Difficult opportunities often require you to confront unfamiliar situations, interact with diverse individuals, or explore new environments. By saying yes to these challenges, you expose yourself to different perspectives, cultures, or ways of thinking. This opens your mind, broadens your horizons, and helps you develop a deeper understanding of the world around you. Embracing opportunities that are hard can lead to

personal and intellectual enrichment that will benefit you throughout your life.

CHAPTER 15

Acknowledge Your Growth

———

In early 2022, I left what many would consider a dream job as general manager of a professional baseball team.

It was a substantial role. A big title as GM and national leadership in my position as a woman in this role. I was good, no, I was great at my job. I loved many areas of my work, but one key area I had the hardest time with was the time away from my family. Working in baseball required a typical 8:30–5:30 plus seventy-two home games per year. I didn't attend them all to the bitter end. I was smart and excluded Sunday games from my contract, so I'd have a steady weekend day at home unless there was an emergency. The season ran from April until early September. Early on, all the work was fun. I loved going to the ballpark. I loved the late nights, entertaining the fans, seeing our team win, and contributing to something big. When we decided to try for a third child, however, I had a feeling those nights of watching 11 p.m. closing fireworks at the ballpark would end.

I had the chance to get the pandemic-delayed season started in early May 2021. Reopening the gates following the pandemic was a moment I'll never forget. I was also nine months pregnant!

I worked nearly every game up until Elin's birth at the end of the month. We were short on staff to start. Many will remember how hard it was to find employees during this period. With all the COVID-19 rules in place, I found myself running downstairs mid-game to take out the trash in the clubhouse. All the single-use items filled the trash faster than the Clubbie could empty, so I hauled up large trash bags to the dumpsters.

It was not glamorous. In leadership roles, you do what you have to do to get the job done, whether it's through management of others or do-it-yourself. I had so many moments during those May 2021 games when I thought about how much I had grown. Eight years earlier, I was at the same stadium with a very pregnant belly—that time with Magnus inside. I was a junior, taking orders, hustling to take care of clients, and building my reputation. This time, I was in charge, running the building alongside the few members of the leadership team. I was proud of myself for how far I had come.

I did feel something different—a certain kind of calm, rather than frantic, during this pregnancy. I had an actual maternity leave on the horizon, my first of my three children. I'd take time off with her and planned to return to work twelve weeks later. Instead of my tight grip on my work, I would let go. I'd let the team do their jobs inside my well-laid plan for my absence. I wouldn't be on calls, come to games, or checkup. I'd be home with my daughter.

I had worked for the team for nearly seven years and was entering a new chapter. Our family had grown to three children, and our careers had blossomed. I spent my summer at home running the boys around to sports, feeding the baby, and sleeping in three-hour intervals. It was beautiful and finite. After twelve weeks off, I'd return to work, and she'd head to daycare. That time came in August with three home stands or eighteen games left in the baseball season.

I returned to work determined to look and act like nothing had changed. I squeezed into the clothes I wore pre-pregnancy, Nike logo polos and Banana Republic work pants. I'd show everyone I was back. I was a leader. I was just like the boys who never had the experience of giving birth, sleepless nights for a mother who awakes to nurse, and C-section recovery. I was here to work.

I showed up each day, finished eighteen more home games of the season, and fought endlessly with my husband, who was essentially a single parent on the nights I worked from eight-thirty in the morning to arriving home around eleven at night with a cooler of pumped milk just in time for Elin's midnight feeding.

Women around the world do this and sacrifice everything to bring home what their family needs. Pretzeling themselves to serve everyone around them. Women are amazing.

I felt like I put on a uniform every morning. Here I was, Emily Jaenson, ready to serve not only this baseball team but women everywhere! I felt I had a rallying cry. I was a martyr. Except no one knew it but me.

However, I was blind to one fact: I was putting work first. I was showing up for my career stronger than my family. I knew something had to give.

I had to stop and examine where my path was taking me and if it was what I wanted.

That year, our family experienced growth. We added a new family member, and our careers and hard work had afforded us the financial rewards we'd been working toward for ten years. I had the space to leave my job, if I chose, and pursue a consulting business to give me the space and freedom to work from home and show up for my family in a way I had not been able to for years.

I was experiencing growth. Leaving a job might feel like a cause for celebration for some, but for me, I wrapped up my entire identity in this role. Who would I be without this business card? Surmounting this hurdle allowed me to grow in so many ways I could not see. I was like a vine who had stretched in one direction, toward work. I had sprouted tiny offshoots of my children, but my main vine kept reaching toward my career. I couldn't see anything but that destination.

Multiple days of reflection and, if I am being honest, fights at home led to me calling it quits. It was a collision of emotions, including confusion, for what would come next. I had experienced change before and knew the right way to get through this was to allow a pause. A chance to acknowledge how far I'd come and to choose where I'd go next.

I sent my last emails as Aces GM in January 2022, bidding farewell to colleagues and partners and finishing my handoffs from my laptop. I had no idea what would come next.

When it came to personal growth, it took me a long time to realize I could do what I wanted with my life. That statement sounds, I don't know, nuts? I found myself living for my career moves and not the life that surrounded me. The family I built. The vacations we should take. My children's youth sports teams I could coach. My excuse for not adding more joy with my family was always work.

Taking this pause allowed me to truly decide what would come next. You have permission to be whoever you want to be at each chapter in your life, and it is your decision alone only dictated by your personal goals. Out of that reflection, I found a way to have everything I wanted.

I didn't figure it out quickly. It took months. I got my first consulting job in May of that year, four months after leaving my job. That same month, I did TEDx. I continued my podcast. I received a call and accepted another consulting job. My TEDx Talk took off, and they offered me a paid speaking gig at the end of the year. Another paid speaking gig in the spring, more would follow.

It's hard to see what's next in your career when you are too busy working with your head down. Difficult situations, like leaving your job without securing a new one, require you to acquire new skills, knowledge, and perspective. In my case the skill was public speaking, knowledge was building a website to market my talents, and the perspective was a shift form team leader to solopreneur. By stepping into unfamiliar territory, you, like me, broaden your horizons and expand your capabilities. This led to personal growth by employing my years-earned skills in a new way, increasing my confidence that I could be an entrepreneur, and opening up new opportunities for personal and professional success.

Today, I have a career as a professional speaker, podcaster, and consultant. You have nearly finished reading my first book. I give myself the gift of reflection to think about how far I have come and fully experience the gratitude that comes along with these thoughts. Give yourself that gift, too. Acknowledge how far you have come, the skills you have learned, and the growth you have experienced. It is from this position we can best align ourselves to determine our next goals.

WHAT GETS IN OUR WAY OF ACKNOWLEDGING OUR GROWTH AND PREPARING FOR OUR NEXT CHAPTER?

In an interview with Ellen Taffe, professor at Northwestern Kellogg School of Management and author of *The Mirrored Door,* she outlined five strategies that help women succeed but also unintentionally sideline them.

1. **Preparing to perfection.** Perfectly preparing can be a tremendous advantage because of the excellence we deliver, but as expectations rise, we don't have time to prepare for

extreme excellence every time. The need to be perfect leads to stress. When you hold yourself to being so perfect in your delivery, you might be micromanaging others, perceiving that you might not be able to take risks, or those around you could think you are not able to deliver without extra time.

How to combat:

1. Step back from your project and ask for help.
2. Use reflection to realize you are more ready than you know (and stop rereading your presentation for the forty-ninth time!).
3. Get help to prioritize. Talk to your boss and understand what projects actually need to be *A+* delivery and which just need to get done.

2. Eagerly pleasing. Being a *pleaser* equates to being a *good girl*. Usually, someone who grew up being *other-oriented* and helpful. In this position, we are advantageous in that we are the glue that holds the team together. This quality is an asset when you can anticipate, read the room, and be a peacemaker. The risk in being a pleaser is we often neglect our own needs. Others can see us as too soft, or others may consider us as someone who can't make tough decisions.

How to combat:

1. Seek respect over likability.
2. Tap into the care we have for others to be straight with them and provide necessary feedback. We can rely on our solid relationships to be better able to inject necessary conflict into that relationship.

3. Set boundaries. Find out where you are in the equation, and if it's not clear, reflect on where you fit in. Don't take everything on yourself, but use your team for their described roles.

3. Fitting the mold. When we take on a leadership position, we can enter the new territory inside a mold to create an ease of understanding of how success looks. Fitting the mold is beneficial when it allows us to ramp up quickly. We can step into the shoes of what that leadership position should look like. The issues arise when we don't show enough of our real self. We rob the team of growth and diversified thinking when we don't share our opinions. It can seed doubt in our own minds when we don't bring our authentic self to work. We think, did they really choose me for this role? We don't see our seat at the table as firm and foundational when we are acting the part.

How to combat:

1. Realize who you are, your strengths, and how you can individually contribute.
2. Understand in reflection that you have earned your seat, and your individuality is necessary to grow the company and your role. Acknowledge your growth!
3. Know you have the right to turn the volume up and down on your authenticity based on the seasons of your life.

4. Working pedal to the metal. A person who is high capacity and hard-charging to get things done is working *pedal to the metal.* This is someone who powers through tirelessly, is goal-focused, can lead others, and makes things happen. It's a successful strategy initially but can become a pitfall when we don't bring others along or burn ourselves out. It is so important to create followers in leadership, but when you are so hard-charging, you may pick up your head, look around, and realize you are alone—you are too far ahead of the team.

How to combat:

1. Share where your motivation comes from and that you are a hard-charging person so your team knows the impact you can have, what to expect, and what they can learn from you.
2. Take time to pause and slow down to bring others along. This builds bonds.
3. Stop and take care of yourself.

5. Performing patiently. When you are heads down, delivering results and waiting for someone to notice, you are performing patiently. Being patient is nice, but as the old adage goes, the squeaky wheel gets the grease. Over time, your boss does not know or understand your ambitions and can pass over you for someone who is making more noise for a promotion. This can breed internal resentment, and other people end up controlling your destiny.

How to combat:

1. Reframe self-promotion as career planning! Get into a conversation with your boss about your ambitions and ask where you're at, where you are in relation to the team, and what you need to do to get ahead.

2. Identify what you want and engage in the dialogue with your boss early and often.[1]

If we can understand these pitfalls, we can better navigate our goals and fully live into and acknowledge our growth. Let's go!

YOU MUST BE INTENTIONAL

In a study conducted by Carina Schroder and Cornelia Nissan, they examined whether the experience of personal growth at work changes over the course of one's career. The nature and content of these challenges seemed to vary according to each person's career phase. This study suggested that you cannot fully understand personal growth independent of a career phase. At some point, personal growth occurs from that which you may have experienced in the past. In other words, depending on the point of our career, we might not know when we are in a period of extreme growth, so be easy on yourself! [2]

In these periods of growth, it's helpful to:

1. Seek help from an advisor, boss, or mentor—someone further along than you—and ask for help. Being alone on the journey is so much harder.
2. Attempt future perspective. When I get there, my future self will think, feel, or act in this way. My future self will thank me for going through this hard time.
3. Extract the lesson along the way. Be an eternal student. When it gets hard, document what you are learning.

4. Reflect on your journey. Where are you now vs. where you were? Do this often. Have coffee with a friend and talk about what's good. Celebrate your success and cheer them on.

I felt pain in leaving my job, but as time does, it healed and revealed. Since exiting that part of my career, in reflection, I am now putting to work my years of experience on a new endeavor. Most importantly, I have fully realized my most precious resource is time. Now, I have more time with my family than I ever thought possible. Growth can be painful, but on the other side is the prize you might not have even known you would win.

You have to get excited about the outcomes. What if you pushed yourself to do something you'd never done before to become more than you ever were? It all starts with awareness. You must acknowledge your growth!

EXERCISE:
1. What is your most precious resource? What do you want more of that you don't have? How will you get it?
2. What is the biggest accomplishment you have had in your personal life? How has it changed you? How has it propelled you forward?
3. What is the biggest accomplishment you have had in your professional life? How has it changed you? How has it propelled you forward?
4. If you acknowledge all the growth you have had in your life (I hope you are smiling), what do you plan to do next?

TOP FOUR TAKEAWAYS:

1. **Development of resilience:** Putting yourself in hard situations exposes you to challenges and obstacles you may not have encountered otherwise. This forces you to adapt, problem-solve, and persevere, ultimately building your resilience and ability to cope with adversity. By pushing yourself outside your comfort zone, you become better equipped to handle future difficulties confidently.

2. **Expanding your capabilities:** Difficult situations often require acquiring new skills, knowledge, or perspectives. You broaden your horizons and expand your capabilities by stepping into unfamiliar territory. This can lead to personal growth by enhancing your overall skill set, increasing your confidence, and opening up new opportunities for personal and professional success.

3. **Increased self-awareness:** Challenging situations tend to reveal your strengths, weaknesses, values, and beliefs: you gain a deeper understanding of yourself in these situations. This self-awareness gives you the opportunity to examine your own thoughts and behaviors and identify areas for improvement. It allows for self-reflection and personal growth as you learn from your experiences and make necessary adjustments to enhance your growth trajectory.

4. **Overcoming fears and building confidence:** Confronting difficult situations enables you to face your fears and insecurities head-on. By pushing through discomfort and taking calculated risks, you prove to yourself you are capable of handling challenging scenarios. As you gradually overcome these obstacles, your self-confidence grows, empowering you to push your boundaries even further. This increased confidence permeates all aspects

of your life and fuels personal growth by encouraging you to take on new challenges and pursue ambitious goals.

Conclusion

————

Whew, we made it! I hope you are as pumped up for yourself as I am for you! You completed a book written to help you grow and change into the best version of yourself. You have thought about and hopefully taken action on all of the prompts offered throughout the book, and you are ready to pick up the pace in creating the life of your dreams.

I broke this book down into chapters with easy-to-apply titles and tactics for a reason. If you ever feel yourself behind in an area, pick this up as a resource. Use the stories of these women to lift you up. Marian Wright Edelman said, "You can't be what you can't see."[1] Here it is, written out for you. Stories of growth and success achieved by everyday women just like you. Let this book join your personal Board of Directors to support you.

I have spent the last three years publishing the podcast *Leadership is Female* as a tool to help you. We have completed over one hundred and fifty episodes and one hundred interviews with highly successful women for one singular purpose: to give back to an incredible community of women who deserve thought leadership.

I took the stage to talk about confidence in front of millions on TEDx, all to inspire the idea that if we practice the behaviors that can lead to attitude change, we can alter our whole lives.

That talk inspired this book, another tool for you to use to grow, evolve, and reach your goals.

Somewhere, a young person is looking up to you. She deserves to see you as the beacon of light that you are. You will show her that with purposeful effort, she can reach her dreams, too.

I will keep showing up for you and for them. However, that's as far as I can take it. I can't make you complete the exercises in this book. I can't make you practice confidence. That is up to you.

Building a big, beautiful life of your dreams is not easy, but I promise you, it is worth it! It means that you are going to have difficult conversations with your coworkers. It means you will have to audibly share your dreams with your partner. It means you will have to set boundaries to carve out time for yourself to accomplish what you have written down as your next goal. It means you can no longer be a wallflower at networking events. You have to show up for your life, and you have to do it in a meaningful way. You deserve it.

We feel stuck without accomplishing our goals, whether small or big. We end up without inspiration, where each day seems monotonous. Doing hard tasks can be scary. When you decide to take action, it means you have to put in effort. But have you ever thought about who you'll be when you finish that journey? The person waiting for you on the other side is amazing. That person is proud and shining with brilliant confidence.

Building a deep, unshakable confidence will help you to succeed in life. Take my word for it!

Bet on yourself. Dig deep. Work hard. Find your *Why*. Practice confident behaviors. Set goals and know you were made for more! I'll always be here to cheer you on.

Let's go!

Acknowledgments

To all the women interviewed on the *Leadership is Female* podcast, thank you! Your willingness to share your story of your career growth in the spirit of helping others was the impetus of this book. You extended a hand back to lead them forward—you didn't pull up the ladder behind you. You shared your how, your why, the hurdles you have overcome, the advice you'd give to the next leader up, and you provided endless inspiration. Thank you for using your voice to help others.

To the women from *Leadership is Female* whose interviews I featured in this book: Odessa "OJ" Jenkins, Jackie Carson, Shauna Griffiths, Jenna Byrnes, Noel Mirhadi, Zaileen Janmohamed, Courtney Rice, Mallory LePage, Rachael DiLeonardo, Larra Overton, Sloane Cavitt Logue, Elisa Padilla, Melanie Newman, Katie Holloway Bridge, Vera Quinn, Jessica Herman, Aubree Curtis, Liz Gray, Shaye Haver, and Ellen Taafee. Thank you for sharing your wisdom!

To those who supported the making of this book during the presale. Your belief in me took my breath away! You only made my efforts feel more valid and worthy. As a result, my confidence in this book grew. Thank you: Randee Hawkins, John Elliott, Keenan Polan, Sarah King, Dr. David Fried, Brooke Ellenberger, Ryan Gilbrech, Corinne Milien, Nicole Gularte, Sara Kepner, Toni Nocita, Brigette Cole, Kelly Wing, Azure Wolf, Nadine Waxenberg, Lindsay Crandall and thank you Lindsay for doing my hair for the cover and author photo—you are so talented, Lindy Deller-Gondoras, Christine Lawrence, Kellie Chung, Mallory LePage, Eric Koester, Allex Nevis, Beth Gorab, Mindy Suszan, Jennifer Emberson, Danielle Peel, Shannon Kelly, Tara Wilson, Amy Haydock, Devon Zeck, my wonderful Sister-in-Law Kim Jaenson, Linda Nunnery, MiLB AGM Jeff Turner, Aunt Paulette Emberson, Lindsay Gaskins, Arielle Moyal, Cindy Santilena, Roger Williams, Beth Weadock, Nicole Williams, Chris Holland, Mother-in-Law Sharon Jaenson, Cherilyn Herzhauser, Karen Triana, Aunt Cindy Opsal, Jennifer Kastenholz, Dad Keith Niles, Abbie Kaucher, Uncle Bob Joyce, Jace Duke, Angela Machado, my amazing husband Shawn Jaenson, Audrey Mollenberg, Paige Hegedus, MiLB GM Erin McCormick, Adam Nuse, Jennifer Luczkowiak, Hannah Michal, Shirley Folkins-Roberts for your unwavering support, Michele LaRocco, Jeff Yocom, Brooke Brumfield, Samantha Hicks, Megan Waddell, Madeline Hamada, Denise Cross for the wonderful teachers at The Goddard School, Sabrina Borghoff, Marilyn Farmer, Lisa Fahey, Amie Sheridan, Kayla Pennington, Emily Reza, Joshua Yonker, Sarah McEwen, Kat Lind, Jen Kelly, Jennifer Wagner, Christina Ghiggeri, Tyler Lind, my big brother Adam Niles, James McGovern, Thomas Calo, Sergio and Amanda Callegari, Abby Johnson, David Benson, Jillian LeBlanc, Kristin McColgan, Dr. Billie Casse, Erika Gruner, Aunt Jeanette Gerke, Kimberly McKinnish with the National Beer Wholesalers Alliance and the Alliance for Women in Beer, Katherine Tartler, Andrea Drew and Cospire at Lake Tahoe who empower women in career, life, and community, my agent Kane Harris, Megan Kurcwal, Tami Powers, Elizabeth Cutri, Pat Barnes, Laura Yurik and the women of ECOLAB, Megan Steigauf, Father-in-Law Richard Jaenson, Shannon Krueger-Karashinski, Jennifer Matthews, Meagan Noin, Fong Menante, Dan Moore, Lesley Klein, Sarah McConnell, Gage Rees, Melanie Jaime, Margaret Kazmierski, and Heather Carranza.

Jeramie Lu from Jeramie Lu Photography for taking my cover photo and author photo. Your talent is so impressive; thank you for documenting the important moments in our lives.

To my brothers, Adam and Peter. Being a middle child of two boys is who I am. You hard-fouled me on the basketball court, windmill-punched me, and used me as a wrestling move dummy. I was always the fastest girl in my class because you chased me. You taught me to be tough, and you showed me how to find the joy in cheering others on ("Go, Z. Go!") as we sat on the sidelines at one another's sporting events for our entire childhood. Today, you still cheer me on, and it means the world to have your support.

To my mom, thank you for everything. Mom, you were so strong, loving, caring, and creative, and you believed in me more than I ever believed in myself. You gave me my first dose of confidence through your unwavering support, and I am forever grateful. I miss you every single day and will spend my life honoring you by living.

To my dad, you instilled in me examples of hard work. You showed me the tangible results of effort. Thanks for all the check-in calls during this writing process. Your continued interest and support in me do not go unnoticed. I still feel like your kid in the game with you cheering me on from the sidelines—much quieter than mom, of course.

Recently, on a podcast interview, someone asked me, "What have been the one to three highlights of your life thus far?" That answer was easy: my children, Magnus, Anders, and Elin. I love you each endlessly and appreciate and cherish all the joy you have brought to my life. I hope I inspire you to chase your dreams with everything you've got and never let anything stand in your way. Live a *big*, confident life. I'll always be here to cheer you on.

My biggest thank you is to my husband. I wanted to write a whole chapter about how you inspire and support me, but I'll keep that between us. From the moment you came into my life, I knew it would change for the better, forever. And it did. We have built an incredible life and family together, one that makes me enjoy the present and look forward to the future. Reflecting on how far we have come has inspired me to keep going, knowing that anything is possible. You support me to pursue all my dreams. You encourage me to dream bigger and go after more. You are my secret weapon. I love you, thank you.

Appendix

___

INTRODUCTION: CONFIDENCE IS A SKILL SET

1. Emily Jaenson, "Six Behaviors to Increase Your Confidence," Spring 2022, Reno Nevada, YouTube Video, 10:12, https://www.youtube.com/watch?v=IitIl2C3Iy8.

2. Emily Jaenson, *Leadership Is Female*, August 23, 2020, https://www.leadershipisfemale.com/.

CHAPTER 1: FIND YOUR WHY

1. The Women's Sports Foundation Report Brief: Her Life Depends on It III (New York: Women's Sports Foundation, May 12, 2015), https://www.womenssportsfoundation.org/articles_and_report/her-life-depends-on-it-iii/.

2. Helen Sharp, "Idea of the Month: You Can't Be What You Can't See," *Ideas Alliance* (blog), June 7, 2018, https://ideas-alliance.org.uk/hub/2018/06/07/idea-of-the-month-you-cant-be-what-you-cant-see.

3. Emily Jaenson, "Sports Illustrated's Most Influential and Powerful Women in Sports, Odessa 'OJ' Jenkins," *Leadership is Female*, September 6, 2021, 43:19, https://podcasters.spotify.com/pod/show/leadershipisfemale/episodes/56—Sports-Illustrateds-Most-Influential-and-Powerful-Women-in-Sports—Odessa-OJ-Jenkins-e16v37q.

4. Ibid.

5. Emily Jaenson, "Sports Illustrated's Most Influential and Powerful Women in Sports, Odessa 'OJ' Jenkins," *Leadership is Female*, September 6, 2021, 43:19, https://podcasters.spotify.com/pod/show/leadershipisfemale/episodes/56—Sports-Illustrateds-Most-Influential-and-Powerful-Women-in-Sports—Odessa-OJ-Jenkins-e16v37q.

6. Ibid.

7. Emily Jaenson, "Finding Your Voice with Jackie Carson, Head Women's Basketball Coach at Furman University," *Leadership is Female*, April 18, 2023, 47:37, https://podcasters.spotify.com/pod/show/leadershipisfemale/episodes/130—Finding-Your-Voice-with-Jackie-Carson—Head-Womens-Basketball-Coach-at-Furman-University-e22b2ps.

8. Ibid.

9. Emily Jaenson, "Do Something That Means Something with Shauna Griffiths, Founder of SLG Impact and CCO at CMD," *Leadership is Female*, February 28, 2022, 47:38, https://podcasters.spotify.com/pod/show/leadershipisfemale/episodes/78—Do-Something-that-Means-Something-with-

Shauna-Griffiths—Founder-of-SLG-Impact-and-CCO-at-
CMD-e1esgoc.

10. Simon Sinek, "How to Discover Your 'Why' in Difficult
Times," April 2021, TED Membership, TEDx Talk, 15:14,
https://www.ted.com/talks/simon_sinek_how_to_discover_
your_why_in_difficult_times?language=en.

11. The Bronfenbrenner Center for Translational Research,
"'Knowing Your Why' Is Good for You," *Psychology Today*,
June 24, 2019, https://www.psychologytoday.com/us/blog/
evidence-based-living/201906/knowing-your-why-is-good-
you.

12. Ibid.

CHAPTER 2: BUILD INTENTION

1. Thomas Webb, PhD, "Building a Bridge Between Intention
and Action or How You Might Start Cycling to Work,"
Psychology Today, September 8, 2016, https://www.
psychologytoday.com/us/blog/the-road-to-hell/201609/
building-a-bridge-between-intention-and-action.

2. Ibid.

3. Thomas Webb, PhD, "Building a Bridge between Intention
and Action—or How You Might Start Cycling to Work,"
Psychology Today, September 8, 2016, https://www.
psychologytoday.com/us/blog/the-road-to-hell/201609/
building-a-bridge-between-intention-and-action.

4. Emily Jaenson, "Succeed in Sales, MiLB, and Family with Jenna Byrnes, Senior VP of the OKC Dodgers," *Leadership is Female*, August 24, 2020, 33.07, https://podcasters.spotify.com/pod/show/leadershipisfemale/episodes/3—Succeed-in-Sales—MiLB—and-Family-with-Jenna-Byrnes—Senior-VP-of-the-OKC-Dodgers-eieb55.

CHAPTER 3: IMPROVE DISCIPLINE

1. Emily Jaenson, "Laser Focus with Noel Mirhadi, Music Talent Agent at UTA," *Leadership is Female*, May 23, 2022, 46:12, https://podcasters.spotify.com/pod/show/leadershipisfemale/episodes/89—Laser-Focus-with-Noel-Mirhadi—Music-Talent-Agent-at-UTA-e1iuo2c.

2. Hub Staff Report, "Susan Wojcicki's JHU Commencement Speech Makes a Splash," University News, *John Hopkins University Magazine*, May 29, 2014, https://hub.jhu.edu/2014/05/29/commencement-wisdom-wojcicki/.

3. Emily Jaenson, "LA28 Olympic Leadership, Zaileen Janmohamed, SVP, Head of Commercial Development & Innovation US Olympic and Paralympic Properties," *Leadership is Female*, November 15, 2022, 50:06, https://podcasters.spotify.com/pod/show/leadershipisfemale/episodes/111—LA28-Olympic-Leadership—Zaileen-Janmohamed—SVP—Head-of-Commercial-Development—Innovation-US-Olympic-and-Paralympic-Properties-e1qovoq.

4. Ibid.

5. Elizabeth Judith, "The Power of Loving Discipline," December 12, 2022, TEDxOcala, 17:02, https://youtu.be/m4rR4mQoWoo?si=qz3G-S9ghCnCKXeV.

6. Ibid.

7. Carol S. Dweck PhD, "Mindset: The New Psychology of Success," (New York City: Random House Group, 2007), 6.

CHAPTER 4: GET UNCOMFORTABLE

1. Rosemary Black, "Glossophobia (Fear of Public Speaking): Are You Glossophobic?" *Psycom* (blog), September 12, 2019, https://www.psycom.net/glossophobia-fear-of-public-speaking.

2. Sujan Patel, "Why Feeling Uncomfortable Is the Key to Success," *Forbes*, March 29, 2016, https://www.forbes.com/sites/sujanpatel/2016/03/09/why-feeling-uncomfortable-is-the-key-to-success/?sh=718ec8b01913.

3. Ibid.

4. Emily Jaenson, "119: Get Uncomfortable and Grow with Courtney Rice, VP of REVELxp," *Leadership is Female*, January 24, 2023, 47:33, https://podcasters.spotify.com/pod/show/leadershipisfemale/episodes/119-Get-Uncomfortable-and-Grow-with-Courtney-Rice—VP-of-REVELxp-e1ttmof.

5. Ibid.

6. Bill Eckstrom, "Why Discomfort Will Ruin Your Life," January 31, 2017, University of Nevada Reno, TEDx YouTube, 12:34, https://youtu.be/ LBvHI1awWaI?si=NeUklggSxWcHNuSW.

7. Ibid.

8. Bill Eckstrom, "Why Discomfort Will Ruin Your Life," January 31, 2017, University of Nevada Reno, TEDx YouTube, 12:34, https://youtu.be/ LBvHI1awWaI?si=NeUklggSxWcHNuSW.

9. Ibid.

10. Bill Eckstrom, "Why Discomfort Will Ruin Your Life," January 31, 2017, University of Nevada Reno, TEDx YouTube, 12:34, https://youtu.be/ LBvHI1awWaI?si=NeUklggSxWcHNuSW.

11. Ibid.

CHAPTER 5: BECOME CURIOUS

1. Francesca Gino, "The Business Case for Curiosity," *Harvard Business Review*, September–October 2018, https://hbr. org/2018/09/the-business-case-for-curiosity.

2. Ibid.

3. Emily Jaenson, "102. Passion Finds Purpose with Mallory LePage, Director of Global Partnerships for the Milwaukee Bucks," *Leadership is Female*, September 13, 2022, 40:40,

https://podcasters.spotify.com/pod/show/leadershipisfemale/
episodes/102—Passion-finds-Purpose-with-Mallory-
LePage—Director-of-Global-Partnerships-for-the-
Milwaukee-Bucks-e1n5sin.

4. Emily Jaenson, "88. Be Curious and Work Hard with Rachael
DiLeonardo, Director of Community and Media Relations
at Midland RockHounds," *Leadership is Female*, May
29, 2022, 45:07, https://podcasters.spotify.com/pod/show/
leadershipisfemale/episodes/88—Be-Curious-and-Work-
Hard-with-Rachael-DiLeonardo—Director-Of-Community-
and-Media-Relations-at-Midland-RockHounds-e1hvjoh.

5. Francesca Gino, "The Business Case for Curiosity," *Harvard
Business Review*, September–October 2018, https://hbr.
org/2018/09/the-business-case-for-curiosity.

CHAPTER 6: DEVELOP CONSISTENCY

1. Emily Jaenson, "HUSTLE with Larra Overton, Host,
Reporter, Producer with the Indianapolis Colts," *Leadership
is Female*, March 1, 2021, 56:30, https://podcasters.spotify.
com/pod/show/leadershipisfemale/episodes/30—HUSTLE-
with-Larra-Overton—Host—Reporter—Producer-with-the-
Indianapolis-Colts-er7j5t.

2. Dan Lier, "How to Create Consistency in Your Life," Dan
Lier, August 10, 2015, YouTube, 6:50, https://youtu.be/
Uvnus5HIInk.

3. Ibid.

4. Marie Forleo, "How to Be Consistent: 5 Steps to Get Things Done, All the Time," Marie Forleo, September 15, 2015, YouTube, 6:52, https://youtu.be/DZNnKzVS1Yw?si=Xauv6QWBw4pEf3ID.

5. Ibid.

6. Isadora Baum, "13 Motivational Quotes from the Rock to Help You Crush Your Workout," *Men's Health*, December 5, 2018, https://www.menshealth.com/entertainment/a25386775/the-rock-motivational-quotes/.

CHAPTER 7: INCREASE SELF-CONTROL

1. Emily Jaenson, "In the Arena with Sloane Cavitt Logue, Talent Agent at WME Nashville," *Leadership is Female*, April 18, 2022, 49:02, https://podcasters.spotify.com/pod/show/leadershipisfemale/episodes/85—In-the-Arena-with-Sloane-Cavitt-Logue—Talent-Agent-at-WME-Nashville-e1h2bt6.

2. Ibid.

3. Melanie Curtain, "In an 8-Hour Day the Average Worker Is Productive for This Many Hours," *Inc. Magazine*, July 21, 2016, https://www.inc.com/melanie-curtin/in-an-8-hour-day-the-average-worker-is-productive-for-this-many-hours.html.

4. Megan Marples, "Decision Fatigue Drains You of Your Energy to Make Thoughtful Choices. Here's How to Get it Back," CNN, April 21, 2022, https://www.cnn.

com/2022/04/21/health/decision-fatigue-solutions-wellness/
index.html#.

5.   Ibid.

6.   K. Anders Ericsson, Michael J. Prietula, Edward T. Cokely,
     "The Making of an Expert," *Harvard Business Review*, July–
     August 2007, https://hbr.org/2007/07/the-making-of-an-
     expert.

7.   Emily Jaenson, "Focus on the Work with Elisa Padilla,
     Award-Winning Sports Marketer," *Leadership is Female*, Dec
     20, 2021, 54:08, https://podcasters.spotify.com/pod/show/
     leadershipisfemale/episodes/69—Focus-on-the-Work-with-
     Elisa-Padilla—Award-Winning-Sports-Marketer-e1bqns7.

CHAPTER 8: ABANDON PERFECTION

1.   Emily Jaenson, "Making It with Melanie Newman,
     Broadcaster for the Baltimore Orioles," *Leadership is Female*,
     April 5, 2021, 46:36, https://spotifyanchor-web.app.link/e/
     FXZR8s3qaEb.

2.   Ibid.

3.   Emily Jaenson, "Making It with Melanie Newman,
     Broadcaster for the Baltimore Orioles," *Leadership is Female*,
     April 5, 2021, 46:36, https://spotifyanchor-web.app.link/e/
     FXZR8s3qaEb.

4.   Charly Haversat, "Perfection Holds Us Back, Here's Why,"
     November 2015, Boston, TED@State Street, 8:27, 2015, https://

www.ted.com/talks/charly_haversat_perfectionism_holds_
us_back_here_s_why?utm_campaign=tedspread&utm_
medium=referral&utm_source=tedcomshare.

5. Tracy Bower, PhD, "Perfectionism Is Bad for Your Career:
   3 Most Important Things to Know," *Forbes*, April 3, 2022,
   https://www.forbes.com/sites/tracybrower/2022/04/03/
   perfectionism-is-bad-for-your-career-3-most-important-
   things-to-know/?sh=2156546be167.

6. Ibid.

CHAPTER 9: DEAL WITH FAILURE

1. Emily Jaenson, "125. 4x Paralympian and NIL Expert, Katie
   Holloway Bridge," Leadership is Female, December 13, 2022,
   47:59, https://spotifyanchor-web.app.link/e/PQs5nqhNbEb.

2. Ibid.

3. Astro Teller, "The Unexpected Benefit of Failure,
   February 2016, Official TED Conference—TED2016,
   TedTalk Video, 17:18, https://www.ted.com/
   talks/astro_teller_the_unexpected_benefit_of_
   celebrating_failure?utm_campaign=tedspread&utm_
   medium=referral&utm_source=tedcomshare.

4. Ibid.

5. Astro Teller, "The Unexpected Benefit of Failure,
   February 2016, Official TED Conference—TED2016,
   TedTalk Video, 17:18, https://www.ted.com/

talks/astro_teller_the_unexpected_benefit_of_
celebrating_failure?utm_campaign=tedspread&utm_
medium=referral&utm_source=tedcomshare.

6. Ibid.

7. Astro Teller, "The Unexpected Benefit of Failure,
    February 2016, Official TED Conference—TED2016,
    TedTalk Video, 17:18, https://www.ted.com/
    talks/astro_teller_the_unexpected_benefit_of_
    celebrating_failure?utm_campaign=tedspread&utm_
    medium=referral&utm_source=tedcomshare.

CHAPTER 10: CHECK YOUR SELF-TALK

1. Emily Jaenson, "Sales Leadership + Winning Mindset
    with Vera Quinn, CEO of Cydcor," *Leadership is Female*,
    October 17, 2023, 40:46, https://spotifyanchor-web.app.
    link/e/1vpY3c1ZoEb.

2. Vasavi Kumar, 2023, "Transform the Way You Talk to
    Yourself in This 8-Week Group Program with Vasavi Kumar,
    November 2, 2023, http://vasavikumar.com/say-it-out-loud-
    group.

3. Ibid.

CHAPTER 11: FIND YOUR PEOPLE

1. Emily Jaenson, "22. Own It! Your Big Career and Your
    Kids with Jessica Berman, Deputy Commissioner for the

NLL," *Leadership is Female*, January 4, 2021, 46:41, https://
spotifyanchor-web.app.link/e/cXNK2FEh8Eb.

2. Ibid.

3. Emily Jaenson, "131. How to Find and Support Your Crew
   at Work, Aubree Curtis + Liz Gray, co-Heads of Global
   Brand Consulting and Social Impact at CAA," *Leadership is
   Female*, April 23, 2023, 46:39, https://spotifyanchor-web.app.
   link/e/ctjvdFGh8Eb.

4. Ibid.

5. Anna Robinson, "Looking for a Mentor? Start by Asking
   These 7 Questions," *Handshake* (blog), Accessed November
   29, 203, https://joinhandshake.com/blog/students/how-to-
   find-a-mentor/.

CHAPTER 12: SET YOUR GOALS

1. Lydia Saad, "Seven in 10 Americans Likely to Set Goals
   for 2023," Gallup, January 5, 2023, https://news.gallup.com/
   poll/467696/seven-americans-likely-set-goals-2023.aspx.

2. Marla Tabaka, "New Study Says This Simple Step Will
   Increase the Odds of Achieving Your Goals (Substantially),"
   Inc., Jan 28, 2019, https://www.inc.com/marla-tabaka/this-
   study-found-1-simple-step-to-practically-guarantee-youll-
   achieve-your-goals-for-real.html.

3. Jeff Boss, "5 Reasons Why Goal Setting Will Improve Your
   Focus," *Forbes*, Jan 19, 2017, https://www.forbes.com/sites/

jeffboss/2017/01/19/5-reasons-why-goal-setting-will-improve-your-focus/?sh=69cb5ef3534a.

4. Tim Ferris, "Why You Should Define Your Fears Instead of Your Goals," April 2017, TED2017, TEDTalk, 13:13, https://www.ted.com/talks/tim_ferriss_why_you_should_define_your_fears_instead_of_your_goals?utm_campaign=tedspread&utm_medium=referral&utm_source=tedcomshare.

5. Ibid.

CHAPTER 13: INCREASE YOUR CONFIDENCE

1. Emily Jaenson, "Six Behaviors to Increase Your Confidence," Spring 2022, Reno Nevada, YouTube Video, 10:12, https://www.youtube.com/watch?v=IitIl2C3Iy8.

CHAPTER 14: SAY YES

1. Oliver Lewis, "More than Half of Brits Are Dealing with 'FOSY'— a 'Fear of Saying yes,'" *Independent*, January 10, 2023, https://www.independent.co.uk/life-style/fear-saying-yes-study-cost-b2259460.html.

2. Ibid.

3. Oliver Lewis, "More than Half of Brits Are Dealing with 'FOSY'— a 'Fear of Saying yes,'" *Independent*, January 10, 2023, https://www.independent.co.uk/life-style/fear-saying-yes-study-cost-b2259460.html.

4. Emily Jaenson, "1st Female Army Ranger Leadership Lessons, Shaye Haver," *Leadership is Female*, August 8, 2023, 55:23, https://podcasters.spotify.com/pod/show/leadershipisfemale/episodes/144—1st-Female-US-Army-Ranger-Leadership-Lessons—Shaye-Haver-e27s45m.

5. Ibid.

6. Emily Jaenson, "1st Female Army Ranger Leadership Lessons, Shaye Haver," *Leadership is Female*, August 8, 2023, 55:23, https://podcasters.spotify.com/pod/show/leadershipisfemale/episodes/144—1st-Female-US-Army-Ranger-Leadership-Lessons—Shaye-Haver-e27s45m.

7. Ibid.

8. *Fortune* Editors, "The World's 50 Greatest Leaders (2014)," *Fortune* Magazine, March 20, 2014, https://fortune.com/2014/03/20/worlds-50-greatest-leaders/.

9. Shonda Rimes, "My Year of Saying Yes to Everything," March 9, 2016, Vancouver, BC, TED Talk, 18:44, https://www.youtube.com/watch?v=gmj-azFbpkA.

CHAPTER 15: ACKNOWLEDGE YOUR GROWTH

1. Emily Jaenson, "Masterclass in Leadership with Ellen Taaffe, Kellogg Professor (Northwestern University) and Author of *The Mirrored Door: Break Through the Hidden Barrier that Locks Successful Women In Place, Leadership is Female,* September 12, 2023, 55:33, https://podcasters.spotify.com/pod/show/leadershipisfemale/episodes/149—Masterclass-

in-Leadership-with-Ellen-Taaffe—Kellogg-Professor-Northwestern-University-and-Author-of-The-Mirrored-Door-Break-Through-the-Hidden-Barrier-that-Locks-Successful-Women-In-Place-e296vq9/a-aalucr9.

2. S. Hommelhoff, C. Schröder, and C. Niessen. "The Experience of Personal Growth in Different Career Stages: An Exploratory Study," Organisationsberat Superv Coach 27, (January 23, 2020): 5–19, https://doi.org/10.1007/s11613-020-00634-y.

CONCLUSION

1. Marian Wright Edelman, "It's Hard to Be What You Can't See," *Child Watch* (blog), Children's Defense Fund, August 21, 2015, https://www.childrensdefense.org/child-watch-columns/health/2015/its-hard-to-be-what-you-cant-see/.

About the Author

———

Praised as a next-level motivator and inspiring leader, Emily lives by her motto, "Be so good they won't forget you!" Her TEDx Talk, "Six Tips for Building Your Confidence," amassed an impressive three million views within a year and ranked number twelve among the 16,000 TEDx Talks uploaded to the YouTube channel in 2022.

Renowned Fortune 500 companies, sports organizations, and national conferences frequently call upon her to speak and consult on creating more confident and goal-driven employees. Emily shares strategies that empower individuals with confidence, reducing fear and anxiety while fostering motivation, resilience, improved relationships, and authenticity in the workplace.

As a pioneer in the sports industry, she made history as the first female General Manager of a Triple-A baseball team in nearly two decades. Emily served on the Major and Minor League Baseball Diversity, Equity, and Inclusion Committee and active participant in front-office inclusion efforts.

Leadership is Female, ranks among the top 2.5 percent globally, and is in the top 200 business podcasts worldwide. It features interviews with female executives, aiming to guide future generations of female leadership.

Emily is a proud wife, a mom of three, and a big fan of the Biggest Little City—her *new* home. She has a giant dog named Thor and a trusty old lab named Remington.